D0526711

INSIDER TIP ▶ Tuscan caviar
The exquisite speciality of the Maremmani lagoon fishermen is bottarga – a hard, amber coloured delicacy of cured roe, mostly from the grey mullet – delicious as an appetizer or grated over pasta → **p. 78**

INSIDER TIP ▶ The Venice of Tuscany
You can experience large parts of Livorno by boat, just as you would in Venice → **p. 81**

INSIDER TIP ▶ Wonderful location
At the Sunset Café in Marina di Pisa you can enjoy a sunset aperitif on the beach or enjoy a nightcap later in the evening → **p. 100**

INSIDER TIP ▶ Live like an artist
A Mexican artist has restored the tiny, idyllic hillside hamlet of Peralta in Camaiore – transforming it into a unique resort with panoramic views over the valley and ancient terraces → **p. 89**

the woodland mountains from the ramparts will take your breath away → **p. 91**

INSIDER TIP ▶ Forgotten river valley
During the Middle Ages a lot more went on in the Lunigiana, in the extreme north-western tip of Tuscany, than today. This is set to change with the revival of the old Via Francigani that winds through the valley of the Magra River → **p. 93**

INSIDER TIP ▶ The bread of the poor
Scientific studies have confirmed what the people of Garfagnana, in Lucca's hinterland, have known for centuries: you can live off the products made from chestnut flour the whole year round without suffering from any deficiencies → **p. 89**

BEST OF ...

FOR FREE

● *Vespa Museum*
In the *Museo Piaggo* in Pontedera, fans of the cult 'wasp' scooters can immerse themselves in its history → p. 101

● *Art in the garden*
Rather than put his money in the bank, collector Giuliano Gori decided to invest in contemporary works by top-class artists and sculptors. The private collection is on display in his landscaped garden, *Fattoria Le Celle* at Pistoia. In the summer the garden is free of charge, but by appointment → p. 45

● *Combine bathing pleasure with cultural delights*
Remember to pack your bathing suit when you visit the Etruscan village of *Populonia* in the Archaeology Park. There you can combine your cultural trip with a swim at the golden sand beach on the *Gulf of Baratti* – one of the most beautiful bays in the region, and there is no entrance fee → p. 83

● *Florentine city oasis*
You will always find a quiet little space between the bookworms and Internet surfers in the *Biblioteca delle Oblate* where you can take a breather or you can enjoy the beautiful view of the cathedral dome from the covered terrace, all for free → p. 39

● *Wellness for free*
The hot springs of *Saturnia* epitomise the wellness world. While hotel guests and day visitors stroll above in white terry cloth gowns, the sulphurous water cascades down into natural rock pools a few hundred feet below, enjoy them at no charge (photo left) → p. 78

● *Princely splendour*
Amongst all the Medici villas around Florence, the *Poggio a Caiano* may well be the most beautiful and is certainly the most elegant → p. 42

○○○○ Dots in guidebook refer to 'Best of ...' tips

● *Picture-perfect Chianti*
Churches and palazzi nestled behind high stone walls and narrow alleys that lead to atmospheric little squares: the picturesque *Radda in Chianti*, is just as you imagined Tuscany to be (photo right)
→ p. 65

● *Vibrant street scene*
During the summer, all over Tuscany, the towns and villages become open air stages with street theatre festivals like the *Mercantia* in Certaldo where fire-eaters, minstrels, acrobats, bands and puppeteers meet up to perform in the streets → p. 117

● *Wind and whales*
Take a *sailing trip* from Viareggio and you may be lucky enough to have some dolphins swim alongside the boat or to spot a whale gliding through the water in the distance → p. 95

● *Agricultural cooperatives*
In the traditionally 'red' Tuscany, farmers and local food producers work together and market their products in cooperative shops, like the *Cantina Vini di Maremma* in Grosseto → p. 73

● *Culinary festivals*
In the length and breadth of the area garish posters announce *sagras*. This is when the town square becomes a restaurant, with the women cooking local specialities and the men and children acting as waiters – and the proceeds mean that the soccer pitch gets a new surface → p. 116

● *Monastic hospitality*
Countless monasteries and pilgrim hospices offer affordable holiday accommodation, for instance *La Verna* in the Casentino and the Franciscan monastery *Domus Bernadiniana* at Massa Marittima → p. 57, 76

● *Engineers of the Iron Age*
The skills and the technical knowledge of the Etruscans deserve our admiration. More than two thousand years ago the lords of Maremma managed cut narrow paths and a complete necropolis and into the soft volcanic rock in the southern Tuscan village of *Sovana* → p. 79

ONLY IN

BEST OF ...

● **Velvet and silk**
The city of Prato owes its fame and fortune to textile production and it now also has a *museum* dedicated to the textile industry and of course it is housed in a converted textile factory → **p. 49**

● **Tuscan underworld**
Caves and copper mines, Etruscan tombs and a medieval sewer system: the cave labyrinth of *Antro del Corchia* at Carrara → **p. 93**

● **Fine chocolates and pralines**
Two or three of his pralines are enough to turn a rainy day into a happy day. An excellent reason for you to visit the shop of the Tuscan chocolate master, *Andrea Slitti*, in Monsummano Terme (photo left) → **p. 46**

● **Remarkable collector**
During his lifetime the eccentric and eclectic Englishman and collector, Frederick Stibbert, turned his magnificent Florentine villa into a type of ethnographical *museum* where he lived amongst his remarkable collection of medieval knights, Japanese warriors, Chinese princesses and Indian maharajas → **p. 112**

● **Monday meetings**
Wine and olive oil are sampled and discussed during the weekly tastings at the biologically managed *Balduccio farm* in Lamporecchio, in the Montalbano hills between Lucca and Florence → **p. 46**

● **Underwater world**
In the *Aquarium* of Livorno, brightly coloured tropical fish flit around the tanks, Otto the giant octopus sucks onto the glass planes and sharks draw in the crowds → **p. 80**

RAIN

RELAX AND CHILL OUT
Take it easy and spoil yourself

● *Divine harmony*
God was a Florentine! And you may well agree with the writer Anatole France, when you enjoy the sun and the panoramic view from the terrace of the *Piazzale Michelangelo* – look down over Florence and see how seamlessly the city and the surrounding nature blend into one another → **p. 32**

● *Relax after your sightseeing marathon*
Swollen feet and an aching back after your long walks and many hours of museums? Then it is time for a wellness break – enjoy an aromatic shower, tropical shower or sauna in the *Hidron* just outside of Florence → **p. 39**

● *Refreshment for the soul*
Take a relaxing canoe trip in nature and glide along past unspoilt river banks with wild birds and grazing horses. A river trip in the stunning *Maremma National Park* is a wonderful way to soothe the soul → **p. 75**

● *Doing sweet nothing*
Just as authentic and unspoilt as the whole Pistoia is, so is its unofficial living room, the historic *Caffè Valiani.* Under fresco-decorated arches you can indulge in coffee, cake and la dolce vita → **p. 45**

● *Spa as a film backdrop*
Simply superb! With the mineral water treatment in the *Tettuccio Terme* in Montecatini you will not only purify your body – the magnificent environment, seen in numerous films, is a sight for sore eyes (photo below) → **p. 46**

● *Getting there is half the fun*
Stroll downhill along the picturesque *Via Vecchia* in Fiesole towards Florence, which spreads itself out in the distance before you. Glorious villas and spacious parks line the way and depending on the time of year, the scent of jasmine and lilies will be everywhere → **p. 41**

INTRODUCTION

DISCOVER TUSCANY!

A street, a house, a church, a blue strip of sky and ocean and in front of that a herd of wild horses. It seems like a fairy tale, but it is reality, according to the popular Tuscan song, 'La mia Terra'. In this ode to the Tuscan home and lifestyle the question is posed: what is it that keeps one coming back? Is it the nature? The art? The history? The lifestyle?

The answer has to be all of the above. A unique blend that makes this central Italian region – between Emilia-Romagna in the north, Lazio in the south, Umbria in the east and the Tyrrhenian Sea in the west – the epitome of beauty and harmony. The Chianti region, between Florence and Siena, particularly reflects this storybook Tuscany with its terraced hills, silvery shimmering olive trees and perfectly laid-out red earth vineyards with stone walls and grazing sheep. And lines of dark green cypress trees,

Photo: Val d'Orcia

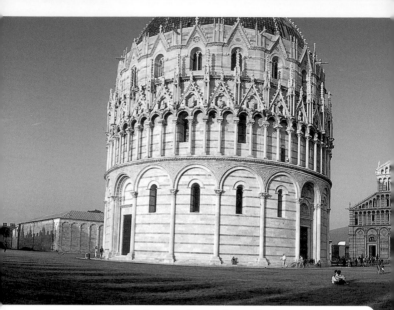

Baptistery, cathedral and (leaning) campanile: the wonderful ensemble of Campo dei Miracoli in Pisa

feudal villas and farmhouses where people come together to enjoy wine and good food in the glow of the setting sun. This is a world from another time and one that stirs the soul.

Nothing has been left to chance in this perfect symbiosis between man and nature. It is a landscape that has been shaped by the people, where generations of farmers and vintners, woodsmen and gardeners, builders and masons have cultivated a rocky, barren wilderness and transformed it into a fertile, terraced landscape. Today the Tuscans preserve their past heritage with the same sense for beautiful form. They have not lost their respect for nature and protect it, as they protect their rich cultural heritage, with strict laws.

10th–6th century BC
Etruscan culture blooms

about 300 BC
The Etruscans lose their supremacy to the Romans

5th–7th century AD
Migration period: the Visigoths, Ostrogoths, Byzantines and Lombards rule successively in Tuscany

From 774
Reign of the Franks under Charlemagne

11th century
The tension between the empire and the papacy splits the cities of Tuscany in two irreconcilable factions: the Guelphs (who supported the Pope) and the Ghibellines (who

This massive region covers more than 8880 square miles and contains an enormous variety of different landscapes. It includes famous regions like Chianti, Maremma, Casentina and the coast of Versilia and its regional differences are immediately obvious when driving through the each area. Coming from the north, you first have to cross over the Apennines, which at some points in the west rise up to 1000m/3280ft high. On the south side the densely forested slopes gradually become gently rolling hills that make up about 70 per cent of the entire region. At times the countryside is a pastoral garden landscape, around Florence or Lucca, then it becomes rough and lunar-like as in the Crete Senesi near Siena, then again it becomes wild and impenetrable as in the Tuscan Colline Metallifere or 'metal hills'. In the west the region extends down to the Tyrrhenian Sea with a coastline that stretches almost 300km/186mi where wide, sandy beaches alternate with sheltered pebble coves and rugged cliffs. On clear days you can see Elba and the other islands of the Tuscan archipelago. The MARCO POLO travel guide for Florence has more detailed information about the region.

However, Tuscany is not only blessed with a beautiful natural landscape – it is also an area awash in art and culture. The 500 museums, 3500 churches, 300 archaeological sites as well as its countless monuments and memorials, make the region one of the richest cultural landscapes of them all. Almost three millennia

Perfect symbiosis between man and nature

supported the Holy Roman Emperor)

12th/13th century
The establishment of the autonomous city republics

1434
Cosimo de' Medici seizes power and sets in motion a three hundred year long family hegemony, first in Florence but later also over the whole of Tuscany

1737
Tuscany falls to Habsburg-Lorraine

1799–1815
Napoleon's Tuscan intermezzo

1860
The nation votes to join the Kingdom of Sardinia

ago, the Etruscans created the first civilisation on the Apennine peninsula. About 2500 years later, the Renaissance heralded the modern age, which made man the measure of all things. This revolution in art, architecture and philosophy attracted artists and architects, amongst them innovators like Giotto, Leonardo da Vinci, Michelangelo, Brunelleschi and Piero della Francesca. They left their mark everywhere, especially in the Tuscan art cities: in medieval Siena, in Pisa (with its famous marble ensemble around the leaning tower), in the elegant and intimate Lucca, protected by its wall, and of course in Florence. Nowhere else will you find as many artworks in such a small area as in this Tuscan city. The whole city is itself a work of art, where every small detail reveals something of its history: from the Romans who founded Florentia, to the free citizens who founded the modern European middle class during the Middle Ages, or the artisans who laid the foundations for the city's fame and fortune with their artistry.

> **The modern European middle class was born here**

Yet, this is still not everything that Tuscany has to offer. If you are interested in the country and its people you should travel along the winding back roads of the Toscana Minore, the Tuscany of little villages and hamlets. Over the years a picturesque landscape has evolved with almost every hill or mountain having Etruscan settlements, Roman fortresses, medieval castles and small villages. Today you can stroll through living history when you explore its narrow alleys and idyllic squares and can enjoy the serenity of the Tuscan way of life with a *gelato* or a glass of wine. The daily afternoon gossip on the bench next to the front door is as much a part of this lifestyle as the card game in the village pub, the evening stroll on the piazza and the annual village festival, the *sagra*, where the residents serve local specialities.

Every village is beautiful in its own way, and all of them are very proud of their history. They even have a term for this: *campanilismo*. The literal meaning of a clannish form of loyalty to your 'bell tower' has disparaging overtones of provinciality, but *campanilismo* still forms the basis for the distinct individualism of the almost 3.7 million Tuscans, who – aware of their culture and their heritage – know that the future has an ancient heart and that progress is always based on tradition.

1865–70
Florence is the capital of the new Kingdom of Italy

1944
The German defence wall in the Apennines runs along the northern border of Tuscany, which thus becomes the battlefield

1999
When Città Slow, a network for environmental protection and quality of life is founded, Tuscany is right at the forefront

2008/2011
A general election confirms a government under Prime Minister Silvio Berlusconi, Tuscany however remains – as with the local elections – a bastion of the left

Of course, there is also the modern day Tuscany that has to deal with the same problems as other regions: traffic jams, air pollution, and environmental sins. But at least these modern issues are kept within limits. Mega-cities, intensive agriculture, industrial centres? Not here! With a few exceptions, like the settlements around Florence, the Tuscans have wisely chosen to live in small, manageable places where

Worth the climb: from the Torre del Mangia you have a magnificent view over Siena

man remains the measure of all things. Be it in everyday life, or in business where medium-sized enterprises and crafts dominate, or in agriculture where the cultivation, breeding and production of quality products are important, one thing above all others remains important: *Piccolo è bello* – small but excellent.

Quality rather than quantity, this Tuscan principle also applies to Tuscany as a holiday region. While there have always been cultural tourists, more and more tourists are being drawn here for relaxa-

> **Here man is the measure of all things**

tion, adventure holidays or for its gourmet delights. It has become a sustainable holiday paradise, where the resources are used cautiously and where, instead of staying in impersonal hotels, tourists can enjoy the *agriturismo*, the Italian form of a farm holiday. In beautifully restored farm estates, country villas and estates with swimming pools and landscaped gardens, the holidaymaker will find the ideal conditions to see, smell and taste the Tuscan world.

WHAT'S HOT

1 Splat, bang, pop

Comics Graphic novels are no longer just for children. Adult comics are true works of art and Italy's comic book capital lies in Tuscany. Not only does the Lucca Comics & Games festival take place here, it is also home to the *Museo Nazionale del Fumetto (Piazza San Romano 4)* comic museum. If you want to browse and buy, visit *Il Collezionista (Piazza San Giusto 1)*. In nearby Pescia, you will find *L'Elefante (Viale Europa 16)*, a library exclusively for comic books.

Natural beauty

2

Wellness Olive oil, sea salt and wine are the beauty enhancers at the *Terme San Giovanni (Via Terme San Giovanni 52, Rapolano Terme)* where nature's ingredients are used in beauty treatments. In *Fonteverde Natural Spa* at San Casciano dei Bagni, the beauty therapists also use nature's bounty just as they do in the *L'Andana Espa (Badiola, photo)*. The secret of the *Spa of the Senses* in the *Terme Sensoriali (Piazza Martiri Perugini, Chianciano Terme)* is their wine therapy – applied externally, of course.

3 Designer palazzo

Old & New In the centre of Florence is the *Una Hotel Vittoria (Via Pisana 59)*. Half palace, half designer hotel, a stay here will set your pulse racing. The *Villa Fortelunga (Via Cunicchio 5, photo)* in Pozzo is more than a hundred years old but there is nothing old fashioned about it. Philip Robinson ensures that iPod docks and antiques go together in perfect harmony. Every visit to the *Gallery Art Hotel (Vicolo dell'Oro 5)* in Florence is different – thanks to the ever changing art exhibitions.

Dancing with the wind

Kitesurfing Once you get the hang of it, this fast-paced wave riding sport is a lot of fun and a good teacher is indispensable when starting to kitesurf. The pros at *Surf Relax (Via Amorotti 2, www.surfrelax.it)* in Follonica will introduce you to the sport or give tips to those who already have the necessary know-how. Further south in Talamone, the kitesurfing school *TWKC (Via Talamonese, www.twkc.it)* offers courses and you can also hire sails, boards and more. If you only need the equipment, you will find it at the *TWKC Shop (Via Aurelia Vecchia 41 m)* in nearby Fonteblanda or at *Hoasy Surf (Via Cestoni 61, www. hoasysurf.it)* in Livorno. In general, the best wind conditions are around Castiglione della Pescaia.

4

No frills

Fiaschetteria Small meals, a glass of wine at the counter and a chat with the bartender or bar lady – this is what you can expect in *fiaschetterie*, the down to earth and authentic wine shops that sell wine and serve homemade and regional specialities. The *Fiaschetteria Nuvoli (Piazza dell'Olio 15)* in Florence is very popular amongst locals because of its affordable prices and good food. If you go further down the small road, you will end up at *La Mescita (Via degli Alfani 70 r)* where they have been serving crispy panini over the counter since 1927. Recently the younger Florentines have discovered this small gastronomical pearl. Outside of Florence there are also *fiaschetterie,* like the *Caffè Fiaschetteria Italiana (Piazza del Popolo, www.caffefiaschetteria italiana.com)* in Siena which has been going since 1888.

5

IN A NUTSHELL

AGRITOURISM

Everywhere signposts point the way to renovated holiday accommodation in picturesque farmhouses and wineries, which are equipped with every possible creature comfort. They often have swimming pools, despite the fact that this region has water problems during the summer. This stylish holiday accommodation now has very little to do with the original idea of guaranteeing small farmers some extra income while at the same time giving nature lovers an authentic insight into farming life. While some farms still produce olives or grapes or have livestock, this aspect is often merely a decorative accessory for the tourism industry which has long since become the main industry. The holiday farm houses from the early days can now be found more on the outskirts of the tourist regions.

ARTIST GARDENS

Tuscany has always drawn artists from all over the world. Fascinated by the rich cultural heritage and the mild climate, many contemporary painters and sculptors have chosen to settle here. They all wanted to realise their dream of a retreat in the countryside where they can work and live peacefully, in harmony with nature. These artists often integrated their art into

Photo: Giglio island in the Parco Nazionale Arcipelago Toscano

In Tuscany – home of the Renaissance – culture is everywhere, it is evident in every aspect of life, from cuisine to architecture

the surrounding nature or created sculpture gardens with their artworks or with those of their friends. The array of current artist gardens range from colourful monuments to a lover or a sound garden where the wind whistles over the sculptures, to landscaped gardens with commissioned works by world famous artists. The majority are open for visitors during summer.

CITTÀ SLOW

Italian word for 'city' combined with the English word slow: Città Slow municipalities are those that have undertaken to go back to supporting traditional structures, to ban cars from the inner city, and to try to use local products and sustainable energy where ever possible. The movement is affiliated to the Slow Food initiative started in 1999, a worldwide movement

It is hard to imagine the original splendour of the tombs: Etruscan necropolis in Populonia

to slow down progress in order to preserve biodiversity and regional specialities. The main aim of Città Slow is to promote liveable, sustainable towns and cities. One of the co-founding members of the movement – which has now gone international – is the small wine producing village of Greve in Chianti.

DOP & IGP

In Tuscany's rolling hills and mountainous regions, intensive agricultural and livestock farming is almost impossible and this is actually quite fortunate given the increasing number of food scares! In order to remain competitive many Tuscan farmers and food producers have started to specialise in high quality local products. The list ranges from chestnut flour from Garfagnana to a particularly tasty poultry breed from the upper Arno Valley, sheep's milk cheese from Pienza and tender ham made from a local breed of pig, Cinta

Senese, from the area around Siena. Typically, all these local products are given a designation of origin or DOP *(Denominazione d'Origine Protetta)*. The DOP guarantees that they have been bred and processed in the traditional way. The specifications for the geographical mark, the IGP *(Indicazione Geografica Protetta)* is not as strict, to obtain the IGP seal any one of the stages of production has to take place within the region of origin.

ETRUSCANS

'The Etruscans, as everyone knows, were the people who occupied the middle of Italy in early Roman days, and whom the Romans, in their usual neighbourly fashion, wiped out entirely in order to make room for Rome with a big R.' This was how the author, DH Lawrence, very drily described the end of the Etruscan nation. It is assumed that the Etruscans originally came from Asia Minor around

1000 BC, and settled in a triangle between the Tyrrhenian coast, Arno and Tiber, but they ceased to exist long before our current era. Nevertheless, the Etruscans where superb builders and craftsmen who left behind permanent traces of their culture. This peace-loving nation, where women were regarded as equal to men, owed their wealth to the mining and processing of iron ore. They also had an unusual cult of the dead. Their cities for the dead – the necropolis – were built for the eternity, their beautiful tombs equipped with everything that would make the afterlife more comfortable. What we know about them today has been learned from the physical legacy that they left behind.

GUELFS AND GHIBELLINES

Sympathetic to the papacy or the emperor – today they would be called middle left or middle right – the opposing factions first emerged around 1215 and are still to this day involved in political disputes. During the Middle Ages, the autonomous city states realised that they could not manage against the expansionism of their neighbours without their mighty patrons. The two factions divided by their loyalties. On the one side were the supporters of the Bavarian dukes of Welf (the Guelfs) who supported the Pope and on the other, the supporters from Waiblingen (subsequently Ghibellines in Italian) who backed the Holy Roman Emperor who promoted the separation of church and power. Florence and Lucca backed the Guelfs because the church favoured trade with their international connections. Arezzo, Pisa and Siena joined the Ghibellines because they hoped for protection against Florentine expansionism. Later the Guelfs started to agree with the Ghibellines who wanted the power to remain with the nobility. The

Guelfs wanted the merchants, who invested in the wealth of the city, to be part of the government. Very soon more importance was placed on which side you supported rather than supporting your own city. This meant that there were often instances when the Ghibellinian Florentines fought on the side of Siena, while the Ghuelfine Sienans fought on the side of Florence.

HISTORICAL GAMES

Many of the Tuscan city festivals have a competitive basis – be it a race or an archery competition – where representatives from the city's neighbourhoods dress up in splendid costumes to compete against each other. The winners are awarded trophies and the games are usually accompanied by magnificent parades as well as feasts and banquets that commemorate events in the city's history. The rather rough ball game Calcio – played in costume in Florence – dates back to a match between Florence and the Imperial troops in 1530. With a few exceptions, like the Palio of Siena, these festivals were long forgotten and only started to gain popularity again during the 1960s.

MAQUIS

As in many other regions in the Mediterranean, Tuscany also has maquis, the low, impenetrable scrub made up of brambles of laurel, broom, juniper, arbutus, heather and myrtle. This was not always so – during ancient times, the whole region was covered in dense forests of oak, beech and pine trees. Many of these forests disappeared due to rigorous deforestation, especially in the coastal regions where Etruscan, Roman and medieval iron works used the wood in the furnaces. The exposed areas were then vulnerable to soil erosion and as a result the robust, evergreen maquis – that flourishes in the dry summer heat – spread out over the countryside.

MEDICI

No other Tuscan family has left a greater mark than the Medici family who rose from humble beginnings as shopkeepers to becoming absolute rulers almost 600 years ago. Originally from Mugello in the northeast of Tuscany, they took over power in the Republic of Florence in 1434 when, as the bankers of the Pope, they became exceedingly rich and influential. Apart from a few small interruptions, they shaped the destiny of this Renaissance city – and later also the whole of Tuscany – for almost 300 years. The Medici were also famous for being patrons of the arts. However, they had ulterior motives in promoting art and architecture. Just as our modern-day sponsorship programmes, their patronage was used as a propaganda tool to increase their power, wealth and fame. In return, the artists received free rein. This made Florence the Mecca for painters, sculptors and architects and the reason why the whole city is one enormous museum today.

MEZZADRIA

Up to the middle of the 20th century a sharecropping system was practiced in Tuscan agriculture. The landowners gave the land, house, livestock, seeds and equipment to a farmer – the mezzadro – who in turn cultivated the land and gave half of their income to the landowner. The landowners lived very well from their half, while the farmers became poorer and poorer. Although land reform in the 1950s enabled many tenant farmers to buy houses, most simply could not afford to do so and were forced to migrate to the cities. Initially, foreigners bought the abandoned farmhouses; today however they are mostly owned by Italians or rented out to holidaymakers.

NATURE RESERVES

Not only are the countless cultural monuments under protection in the traditionally left-ruled Tuscany, but there are also large tracts of natural landscape – a good ten per cent of the territory, almost 850 square miles – far more than any other region in Italy. There are two national parks: the Parco Nazionale Arcipelago Toscano, the largest marine reserve in the Mediterranean, and the Parco Nazionale delle Foreste Casentinesi with its enormous forests of trees, beautiful waterfalls and diverse fauna. In addition, there are more than 100 other local and regional parks and protected reserves. They usually all have a visitors' centre with detailed information and maps.

PIEVE

It is no coincidence that the small, simple churches, which are amongst the oldest examples of Tuscan sacred architecture, are located outside the villages. From the 11th century they were built along the most important routes so that both residents and travellers could easily access them. They were mostly parish churches, recognisable by having their own baptismal font and cemetery. Built using local materials – roughly cut stones, timber and terracotta – they have the simple layout of early Christian basilica with an open roof truss nave that extends behind the choir in the apse and they were also often without a transept.

RENAISSANCE

The Renaissance – rinascita in Italian – was a cultural movement that saw the rebirth of ancient ideals in philosophy, science and art. The painter and architect, Giorgio Vasari, coined the term for the period between 1400 and 1600 when this profound cultural change took place. During the Middle Ages the church had the monopoly on education which meant that the dominant world view centred around God. The Florentine humanist, Francesco Petrarch, branded this period as 'dark' and instead proposed a more secular approach that included an appreciation of worldly pleasures, a world in which man was the measure of all things and an assertion of personal independence and expression. Inspired by this humanist approach, artists once again showed worldly pleasures in their

WINE ROUTES

That Tuscany is also the country of culinary culture is evidenced by the no less than 15 wine routes that meander through the Tuscan countryside. As the name suggests, everything centres on wine. Brown road signs indicate the wine estates, cellars and wine tasting venues. But there is no shortage of other culinary specialities and cultural monuments. For instance, the Strada del Vino Vernaccia di San Gimignano attracts visitors for the

The Neptune on the Piazza della Signoria in Florence bears a resemblance to Cosimo I. de' Medici

paintings and instead of rigid representations, they now focused on a more true to life depiction of people and landscapes. At the same time Gothic architecture, with its church towers that reached up to the heavens, was replaced with Renaissance architecture that had an emphasis on symmetry, proportion and horizontal lines.

saffron that is cultivated in the region while the Strada del Vino Costa degli Etruschi shows how cold pressed olive oil is produced. The Strada del Vino Nobile di Montepulciano makes a detour to the thermal springs in Bagno Vignoni, and chestnut products from the forests of Monte Amiata are amongst the attractions of the Strada del Vino di Montecucco.

FOOD & DRINK

The guiding principle of traditional Tuscan cuisine is to use only a few ingredients but they need to be of the very best quality. The food is not overly refined; the emphasis is rather on the taste of each separate ingredient in the dish.

Tuscan cuisine uses fresh regional produce and, just like a farm kitchen, whatever is found seasonally in the garden, stable or forest, is served at the table. The most important ingredient is cold pressed olive oil and animal fats are seldom used. In Tuscany the much vaunted Mediterranean diet is the most natural thing in the world. Antipasto, primo, seconde, dessert: eating all the dishes does not happen that often

in Tuscany anymore. Nowadays it happens when people have guests over, when friends and colleagues meet up in restaurants or on festive days when the whole family is gathered around the table. Meals are always accompanied by bottles of *acqua minerale*, either *liscia* (still) or *gasata* (with gas), local red wine *(vino di casa)* and bread made without salt. Because with all the aromatic herbs and fresh flavours, you do not need any salt.

For *prima colazione* (breakfast), pastries and coffee are preferred, usually in the bar on the corner so avoid the boring breakfast buffet in the hotel and do as the locals do but remember to only order an

Top quality, fresh basic ingredients are the cornerstone of Tuscany's delicious – and healthy – cuisine

espresso con latte caldo or cappuccino – or else you will be served instant coffee *(caffè americano)* as a caffè latte.

Antipasti are meant to keep guests happy while they wait for the freshly prepared meal. Typical in Tuscany are *crostini* or bruschetta with vegetables pickled in oil, *prosciutto* with melon or a *pinzimonio,* mixed raw vegetables with olive oil. This is followed by the *primo piatto*, the first course, usually pasta or, typically in Tuscany, a hearty vegetable soup. The main course, the *secondo*, consists of fish or meat; a salad or vegetable side dish *(contorno)* if desired. This is rounded off with fruit, sheep's milk cheese or *cantuccini*, hard almond biscuits from Prato, which are dunked in the *vin santo* dessert wine.

If you love ice cream, you will be in heaven as there are *gelateria* everywhere in

LOCAL SPECIALITIES

▶ **aglio, olio, peperoncino** – minced garlic and chillies in cold pressed olive oil – unbeatable as a pasta sauce

▶ **arista alla fiorentina** – roast pork, seasoned with garlic and rosemary

▶ **bistecca alla fiorentina** – T-bone steak (the best is Chianina beef from the Chiana region) the meat is cooked on a charcoal grill and then seasoned and brushed with olive oil

▶ **bollito con salsa verde** – mixed cooked meat (chicken, beef, tongue ...) with a sauce made from herbs and olive oil

▶ **bruschetta** – toasted white bread brushed with garlic, salt, olive oil and eventually tomato (photo left)

▶ **cacciucco alla livornese** – creamy fish soup made from everything that the sea has to offer

▶ **castagnaccio** – cake made from chestnut flour with pine nuts and rosemary

▶ **crostini** – toasted white bread, often with chicken liver pâté

▶ **fagioli all'uccelletto** – white beans in tomato sauce with sage

▶ **panforte/panpepato** – spiced Christmas cake with almonds and candied fruit – from Siena

▶ **pappa col pomodoro** – a primo of tomato sauce and stale bread

▶ **peposo** – Tuscan veal stew with lots of black pepper and red wine

▶ **pici** – thick durum wheat noodles, good with a hearty meat sauce

▶ **pinzimonio** – carrots, fennel, celery sticks dipped raw in a mixture of olive oil and salt

▶ **ribollita** – soup of white beans, cabbage and soup vegetables, best eaten on the day after it is made (photo right)

▶ **trippa alla fiorentina** – veal tripe with tomato sauce and soup vegetables

▶ **zuppa di farro** – spelt soup with soup vegetables and kale

Tuscany. Look for the *artigianale* (home made) sign and watch out if the ice cream is piled high as that is a sure sign that it contains all sorts of additives. In tourist centres, fixed price menus *(menú turistico)* are often on offer but if you prefer not to have a set menu, you will need to spend a little more. In addition there is the *coperto*, a flat charge for cover and bread. The *servizio*, a service charge, is usually included in the price of the meal. Tips are only given if you are satisfied with the service.

Chianti: the classic amongst the Tuscan reds

The distinctions between the different types of restaurants – *ristorante, trattoria, osteria, pizzeria, rosticceria, enoteca* – are often blurred and the different price categories are of no help either. If you want to avoid any uncomfortable surprises it is best to first check the menus that are posted outside the restaurant.

There are bars on almost every corner where locals start the day with a cappuccino and a *brioche*, a croissant or other types of sweet pasty. In the afternoons they serve sandwiches (*panini* or triangular *tramezzini*) with salad and at night you can enjoy an *aperitivo*. Although the drinks might be more expensive at this time, you may however, enjoy the finger food buffet for free while the *pasticcerie* has the cakes and pastries that guests often take along to evening dinner invitations.

Seven DOCG, 36 DOC, and six IGP: this is how Tuscany promotes its wine industry. The region tops the list of Italian quality wines that have the controlled, or controlled and guaranteed, seal of approval. And that is only the tip of the iceberg – or rather the vineyard – because in the over 40 cultivated regions, some top wines like the Sassicaia (one of the legendary prize-winning 'Super Tuscans') hide behind the *vino da tavola* category. A tip if you are uncertain: look for *prodotto e imbottigliato all'origine* on the label, this means that the wine was bottled by the grower and the vintner uses his name as a guarantee of quality.

Tuscany traditionally produces red wines, Brunello di Montalcino, Vino Nobile di Montepulciano, Chianti Classico and more recently Morellino di Scansano are the bestsellers of the region. They all have one thing in common, the Sangiovese grape, an old Tuscan grape varietal.

However, white wines are also very popular, especially the dry and fruity Vernaccia di San Gimignano from another typically Tuscan grape variety. In general, the other grapes grown in the region have come from elsewhere, like Merlot, Cabernet Sauvignon or the famous Sardinian white wine variety Vermentino, the current star of the Tuscan white wines.

The sweet *vin santo* is an excellent Tuscan dessert wine. The white grapes are hung in a well ventilated room, dried and stored for at least three years before use.

SHOPPING

There is no better place than Tuscany to indulge in some retail therapy, after all it does have rather a long tradition of great style and artistic flair.

ACCESSORIES

Italian elegance is very evident in the small things: the refined scarf, the gorgeous hat, the hand crafted shoes, the unusual costume jewellery, and embroidered napkins for the festive table. The stylish Tuscans are surrounded by beauty and they know exactly what fits best with what. If you can afford it, it is best to purchase your accessories either from a traditional speciality shop or from one of the luxury boutiques of the top international fashion designers. However, you can be very creative even with a modest budget: look in the local *mercerie* (haberdashery) stores, as well as in the large department stores like Coin, La Rinascente or Upim and sometimes even on the rummage tables at the weekly market. All you need here is just a bit more time.

CRAFTWORK

Arte and *arti* – art and handcraft – the Italian language has them as two sides of the same coin and this region has been famous for centuries for its skilful workmanship of leather, paper, and terracotta, gold and marble. These old skills are handed down from generation to generation and in addition to the traditional crafts – picture frame gilding, making mosaics and hand painting ceramics – there are also contemporary crafts that combine tradition with the spirit of the times. In small boutique workshops, botteghe, Tuscan masters still create their master pieces today and you should try to make some time to watch them while they work. When you see the care and skill in their craft you will then understand that quality has its price.

CULINARY

Every area, and almost every village, in Tuscany has its own culinary speciality: chestnut flour from Garfagnana, *lardo* (bacon fat) from Colonnata cured in mar-

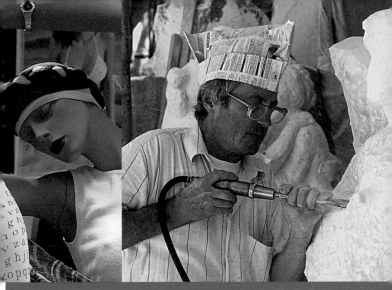

Tuscany is the source of many fine things –
buy yours at the markets, the wine shops,
the department stores or the outlet centres

ble vats in the Apuan Alps, pecorino from Pienza, chocolates from Monsummano Terme … these are the travel souvenirs most popular with Italians. You need never look very far, not even in the most remote corner, for a delicatessen or farming cooperative that makes or sells these tasty culinary souvenirs. Even the large supermarket chains, such as Coop, have sections with specialities from the region. However, the best place to shop is at the farmer's market on weekends where vegetable farmers, shepherds and livestock farmers from the surrounding area offer their products. Regional wine can be bought at wine shops *(enoteca)* and *vino sfuso* in the smaller shops and of course directly at the producers but bear in mind that the unsealed *vino sfuso* does not travel well.

FASHION & MARKETS

Milan has long since replaced Florence as the country's fashion capital. Yet, it was Tuscan labels such as Gucci, Pucci, Prada and Ferragamo that made Italian fashion famous. But the city of Arno is catching up again – and Tuscan creativity is once again at the forefront. Everywhere young stylists are setting up their own studios and making limited edition items, the fashion streets in the Tuscan city centres are always right on trend with the latest fashions – and often a season ahead of other European cities. If you cannot afford the alta moda, you need only be a little patient. At the end of the season the creations are sold off at the weekly markets or in one of the many outlets that are often conveniently situated next to motorway exits, or on the outskirts of town, and are the modern places of pilgrimage for families during weekends.

THE PERFECT ROUTE

CULTURE AND THE COAST

Start with a dose of culture in ❶ *Pisa* → p. 96 on the world famous Piazza dei Miracoli (photo left) around the leaning tower and in the medieval old town. There will still be some time left for a trip to ❷ *Viareggio* → p. 95, to enjoy the sunset on the beautiful seaside promenade.

ELEGANT CITIES IN THE NORTH

A short stretch of motorway separates Viareggio from ❸ *Lucca* → p. 84, and you should plan half a day to explore this picturesque walled town. In the afternoon you can go to the elegant ❹ *Montecatini* → p. 46 with its magnificent spa gardens and thermal baths, where you will experience a touch of the belle époque. Then on the next day there are two cities that live in Florence's shadow. The first is ❺ *Pistoia* → p. 43, where a stroll through the beautiful old town is a must and then – after a light lunch in the Caffè Valiani – the textile city ❻ *Prato* → p. 48, where its ancient walls conceal a true gem.

FABULOUS FLORENCE

Schedule a full day for the cradle of the Renaissance and then – once you have completed the obligatory cultural tour of the cathedral, Palazzo Veccion and the museums of your choice – stroll through ❼ *Florence's* → p. 32 alleys and soak up the atmosphere.

THROUGH CHIANTI TO SIENA

In the evening head towards ❽ *Greve in Chianti* → p. 65 and almost any place in the Chianti region between Florence and Siena, is worth a stop but do not give in to temptation too often, because just on the other side of the Florence-Siena motorway is the magnificent medieval ❾ *San Gimignano* → p. 68 and the Etruscan town ❿ *Volterra* → p. 68 built on porous volcanic rock it is on to the next stop: ⓫ *Siena* → p. 60, a red-brick and stone medieval marvel of atmospheric alleyways and fascinating buildings.

CASTLES, MONASTERIES, FORESTS IN THE EAST

Just over 90km/50mi away is ⓬ *Arezzo* → p. 52 where you can see the famous frescoes of Piero della Francesca and bask in culture as

Experience the facets of Tuscany on an extended roundtrip from the coast through forests and wine lands and back to the beaches

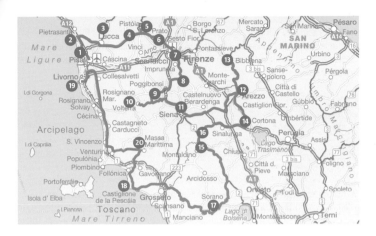

you sit at a restaurant table on the Piazza Grande with its wonderful atmosphere. Arezzo is the ideal start for a trip to Casentino with the medieval fairy castle in ⑬ *Poppi* → *p. 59*. A winding road takes you from there to the monastic silence of Camaldoli which should give you the boost of energy you need to go some 70km/ 43.5mi south to ⑭ *Cortona* → *p. 58*, to finish the day on the central piazza.

WINE AND ETRUSCAN VILLAGES IN THE SOUTH

From Cortona its only a short stretch to the wine producing town of ⑮ *Montalcino* → *p. 66*, where the smell of Brunello is everywhere. Take the road via Asciano right through the hilly landscape of Crete, and past the lovely abbey ⑯ *Monte Oliveto Maggiore* → *p. 64*. ⑰ *Sorano, Sovana and Pitigliano* → *p. 78, 79* are all very Etruscan in character, from here it is not far to the Maremma coast with the magical ⑱ *Castiglione della Pescaia* → *p. 74* (photo below).

BACK TO THE COAST

The last stage (170km/105mi) is to the port city ⑲ *Livorno* → *p. 79*, where the Tuscans show their more modern side. Even though it is a short stretch it is best to plan on taking a whole day for this trip, because along the way you will find the medieval work of art, the ⑳ *Massa Marittima* → *p. 76* as well as the equally delightful Campiglia Marittima.

About 900km/560mi. Recommended travel time: at least (!) eight days. Detailed map of the route on the back cover, in the road atlas and the pull-out map

FLORENCE & THE NORTH

As diverse as the three provinces of the north-east are – Florence rooted in its past, commercial Prato and peaceful Pistoia – together they form the political and economic centre of Tuscany. Their wealth has come through trade and workmanship, their fame through art, culture and the unique beauty of the landscape.

FLORENCE

▨ MAP INSIDE BACK COVER
(138 C6) (*ΩΩ J–K8*) During 1817, the French writer Stendhal wrote a travel article in which he warned that Florence can

🏙 WHERE TO START?
The ● ☼ **Piazzale Michelangelo (U E6)** is the perfect place get an overview of the city, the best option is to take bus number 13 or a train straight to the Piazzale and its panoramic views. A stairway leads you from there to the Oltrarno, a part of the city that is full of craft workshops. From there you can go over the famous Ponte Vecchio bridge, into the city centre with its famous landmarks; the Palazzo Vecchio, the Duomo and the Basilica Santa Croce.

Photo: Galleria degli Uffizi in Florence

Urban landscapes as works of art: in and around Florence, Prato and Pistoia, beauty and quality of life are very much at home

make you ill – this was after he collapsed here from sheer art exhaustion. During the 20th century a Florentine psychiatrist diagnosed this reaction as the 'Stendhal Syndrome' when dozens of visitors to Florence suffered a similar reaction.

There is nowhere else that will you find so much art in such a small area than in this city (370,000 inhabitants) on the river Arno where, in the 14th century, the Renaissance heralded a new age of philosophy, art and architecture. Not only is it an open air museum but it is also a city of shopkeepers and craftsmen. During the day the city is full of the sounds of artisans hammering and sawing in workshops. During the evening the city is also alive, as bars and restaurants put their tables out in the street and fun lovers travel from the one venue to the next.

Brunelleschi's mighty cathedral dome dominates Florence's skyline

SIGHTSEEING

CATHEDRAL, BAPTISTERY AND CAMPANILE (U C3)

The octagonal baptistery, the *Battistero San Giovanni (Mon–Sat 12.15pm–7pm, Sun, 1st Sat 8.30am–2pm | 4 euros)* with its Byzantine mosaic ceiling and unique bronze portals, was consecrated in 1059. In 1296 the citizens decided to build a cathedral, the *Duomo Santa Maria del Fiore (Mon–Wed and Fri 10am–5pm, Sat 10am–4.45pm, Sun 1.30pm–4.45pm, Thu 10am–4.30pm, May and Oct 10am–3.30pm, July–Sept 10am–5pm | free admission)* next to it. But it was nearly 150 years later, that the building master Filippo Brunelleschi, succeeded in closing the opening of the building with the ★ ☆ *dome (Mon–Fri 8.30am–7pm, Sat 8.30am–5.40pm | 8 euros)*. By that time the Giotto's bell tower, the ☆ *Campanile (daily 8.30am–7.30pm | 6 euros)* was long finished. Behind this multicoloured marble building is the cathedral museum *(Museo del Duomo | Mon–Sat 9am–7.30pm, Sun 9am–1.45pm | 6 euros)* housing treasures from all three buildings. *www.operaduomo.firenze.it*

GALLERIA DELL'ACCADEMIA (U D2)

This is where you will find the star of the history of art – Michelangelo's David (the much-photographed sculpture on the Piazza della Signoria is only a copy) – with the famed head wreathed ivy and the proud muscular body turned slightly to the left. But there are many more high-calibre works of art on show here. Advance booking is recommended *(tel. 0 55 29 48 83). Tue–Sun 8.15am–6.50pm | 6.50 euros plus 4 euros for ticket reservation | Via Ricasoli 60 | www.polomuseale.firenze.it*

GALLERIA DEGLI UFFIZI ★ (U C4)

In 1560 Cosimo I de' Medici commissioned Giorgio Vasari to build this u-shaped building for the officials of the Republic of Florence. His successor established an art gallery in the upper floor, which was constantly enlarged and today the Medici's cultural and artistic legacy takes up 45 of its rooms. Included are Sandro Botticelli's Allegory of Spring, Leonardo da Vinci's Annunciation and Filippo Lippi's Adoration of the Magi. Advance booking recommended *(tel. 0 55 29 48 83). Tue–Sun 8.15am–6.50pm | 6.50 euros plus 4 euros for ticket reservation | Piazzale degli Uffizi | www.polomuseale.firenze.it*

MUSEO NAZIONALE DEL BARGELLO ★ (U D4)

The oldest public building in Florence, it was built in 1255 by the free citizens of the Republic of Florence for the *podestà*, the city magistrate. Today this fortress-like building houses a large collection of Renaissance sculptures. *Daily 8.15am–5pm, 1st/3rd/5th Sun, 2nd/4th Mon closed | 4 euros | Via Proconsolo 4 | www. polomuseale.firenze.it*

MARCO POLO HIGHLIGHTS

PALAZZO PITTI ★
AND GIARDINO DI BOBOLI (U B5–6)

During the 15th century the merchant, Luca Pitti, wanted to build the largest palace in the city on the left side of the river. He went bankrupt and had to watch as his worst enemies, the Medici family, built it up to its current size. The palace is large enough to house six museums, including the Galleria *Palatina (Tue–Sun 8.15am–6.50pm | 8.50 euros | Piazza Pitti)* behind it lie the *Boboli Gardens (April/May/Sept/ Oct daily 8.15am–6.30pm, June–Aug 8.15am–7.30pm, Nov–March 8.15am–4.30pm, closed 1st and 4th Mon | 7 euros)* which were laid out in 1550. The gardens have flower beds, ornamental gardens, grottoes and pergolas. The entrance ticket for all museums costs 11.50 euros and is valid for three days.

PALAZZO VECCHIO (U C4)

For 700 years the palace at the Piazza della Signoria has been the centre of secular power in Florence. During the Middle Ages, the castle-like building housed the elected representatives of the Republican city government and in 1540 Cosimo I de' Medici made it his residence. Since 1872 it has been the seat of the city council. Walk through the richly decorated *Cortile Michelozzo* to reach the massive, fresco-decorated Hall of the Five Hundred *(Salone dei Cinquecento)* and the private chambers of Eleonora di Toledo on the first floor. *Thu, Sun 9am–2pm, otherwise 9am–7pm | 6 euros | www.museicivicifiorentini.it*

PONTE VECCHIO 〰 (U C4–5)

The bridge, with its three stone arches and its pastel coloured buildings, links the two banks of the Arno where trade flourished during the Middle Ages. Running above the bridge is *Vasari's Corridor*, build so that the Medicis could move freely between their residence and the Palazzo Pitti.

SAN LORENZO
AND CAPPELLE MEDICEE (U C3)

The bronze pulpits and sculptures by Donatello are one of the reasons why the Medici's parish church *(Mon–Sat 10am–5pm, Sun 1.30–5.30pm | 3.50 euros | Piazza San Lorenzo)* is regarded as one of the most splendid sacred buildings in the city. Master builder and architect Filippo Brunelleschi created a Renaissance jewel with the old sacristy. A back door from

LOW BUDGET

▶ In Tuscany there are a lot of centrally located Christian guest houses that are a far cry from being monastic but as they are so reasonable you do have to book well in advance. One example is the *Istituto Gould (Via de' Serragli 49 | tel. 0 55 21 25 76 | www. istitutogould.it)* in Florence, where you can get an en suite double room for 50 euros.

▶ At Pino in the *Enoteca Verdi (Mon–Sat 8.30am–8pm | Via Verdi 36 | tel. 0 55 24 45 17)* in Florence you have to choose your own panini, primo and secondo from the counter (unfortunatly also served on plastic plates) but the food is tasty and affordable: everything costs less than 5 euros!

▶ Prato is a bargain hunter's paradise where you can find (almost) everything in the factory at half price: cashmere pullovers, underwear, leather goods ... for a list of shops and factories click on the 'Where to Shop' section *www.prato turismo.it/index.php?lang=en* the Piazza Madonna degli Aldobrandini leads through to the splendid marble mosaics of the Medici family tombs in the *Cappelle Medicee (summer daily 8.15am–4.50pm, winter 8.15am–1.50pm | 6 euros | www.polomuseale.firenze.it)*. Their sculptures, as well as the new sacristy behind them, were made by Michelangelo.

SAN MINIATO AL MONTE ☼ (0)

This church *(summer daily 8.30am–7pm, winter 8am–12.30pm and 2.30–7.30pm)* with its cemetery is visible from afar as it is on a hill south of the Arno River. The interior is a treasure of Romanesque architecture with frescoes and marble inlays in the floor. *Mon–Sat 8.30am–7pm, Sun 8am–12.30pm and 2pm–7pm | Via Monte alle Croci*

SANTA CROCE ★ (U D4)

The Franciscan order commissioned this massive church in 1295. They also commissioned artists to paint the founder of their order and the Gospel for the faithful on the walls. Amongst the painters was Giotto, the pioneer of the Renaissance. In his frescoes he used blue instead of gold and, unlike the Byzantine artists, gave his figures natural body shapes, and gave them expressions which showed them smiling or crying. It was the first step to a type of art that focused on naturalism. *Mon–Sat 9.30am–5.30pm, Sun 1–5.30pm | 5 euros | Piazza Santa Croce 16 | www.santacroceopera.it*

INSIDER TIP SPEDALE DEGLI INNOCENTI (U D3)

The babies depicted on the terracotta medallions on the exterior façade of the Della Robbia reveal the purpose of the building as Italy's oldest foundling hospital (now a museum) where babies could be anonymously deposited in a baby hatch. Built in 1445 by Filippo Brunelleschi the building

The view makes the climb up San Miniato worthwhile

was a front-runner of the horizontal building style of the Renaissance. *Daily 10am–7pm | 5 euros | Piazza Santissima Annunziata 12 | www.istitutodeglinnocenti.it*

FOOD & DRINK

TRATTORIA LA CASALINGA (U B5)

The name says it all: here you get typical Tuscan home cooking at moderate prices. But the word is out – so now you may have to wait awhile in the evenings for a free table. *Closed Sun | Via dei Michelozzi 9 r | tel. 0 55 21 86 24 | Moderate*

TRATTORIA IL CONTADINO (U A3)

During the afternoons it is difficult to get a seat in this simple trattoria (with a fixed price menu) but at night the local crowd makes way for the tourists. *Closed Sun | Via Palazzuolo 71 r | tel. 05 52 38 26 73 | Budget–Moderate*

ROCCO E I SUOI FRATELLI (0)

A simple trattoria with a summer garden where you can enjoy reasonably priced and delicious pizzas. *Closed Tue | Piazza Ravenna 10 | tel. 0 55 68 58 02 | Budget*

IL SANTO BEVITORE (U B4)

Fresh ingredients, good wine and friendly people all make this restaurant in trendy Oltrano a favourite meeting place for both locals and tourists. *Closed Sun | Via Santo Spirito 64 r | tel. 0 55 2112 64 | www.ilsanto bevitore.com | Moderate*

SHOPPING

FIERUCOLA ⏱ (U B5)

On the third Sunday of the month, Florentines spoil themselves with organic products from the surrounding region at this farmer's market. *9am–7pm | Piazza Santo Spirito | www.lafierucola.org*

INSIDER TIP ▶ MAESTRI DI FABBRICA (U D4)

Knives from Scarperia, copper pans from Pistoia, exclusive handbags from Scandicci: here you can find top quality products from the best Tuscan workshops. *Borgo degli Albizi 68r | www.maestridifabbrica.it*

FASHION

Names like Gucci, Ferragamo, Cavalli, Pucci, Patrizia Pepe and Prada are all testimony to Tuscan elegance and their luxury boutiques are in *Via Tornabuoni, Via della Vigna Nuova* and *Via Roma* (U B–C 3–4) while areas like Santa Croca and Santa Spirito are the domains of the smaller labels like *Poncif* ((U D4) *| Borgo degli Albizi 35 r | www.poncif.com)* and *Quelle Tre* ((U B4) *| Via Santo Spirito 42 r | www.quelletre.it).*

SIMONE TADDEI (U C4)

His calf's leather photo frames and cigarette cases go through about 30 steps to burnish the leather so that they look as though they are made from wood. *Via Santa Margherita 11*

Top designers like Pucci, Gucci and co. in Via Tornabuoni and its side streets

VESTRI (U D4)

The chocolate king of Florence. *Borgo degli Albizi 11 r | www.vestri.it*

SPORTS & ACTIVITIES

Florence even has its own beach, at *Spiaggia sull'Arno* on the *Lungarno Serristori* (U D5) from mid-June to the end of September – even if it is just for sunbathing. For the more active there is *Florence by Bike ((U C2) | Via San Zanobi 120/122 r | tel. 0 55 48 89 92 | www.florencebybike.it)*. A special kind of summer fun is a trip on the Arno in a flat bottomed barchetti boat steered by a renaioli *(12 euros/per hour | reservations essential at tel. 34 77 98 25 66 | www.renaioli.it)*. The largest wellness and sports park is the ● *Hidron Fun Sport ((138 B5) (ⓜ J7) | Campi Bisenzio | Via di Gramignano, | www.hidron. it) just outside of town.*

ENTERTAINMENT

INSIDER**TIP** ► **BIBLIOTECA DELLE OBLATE** ● (U D4)

Enjoy a view of the cathedral and an aperitif as you read or surf the Internet. *Mon–Sat 9am–midnight | Via Oriuolo 26 | www.bibliotecadelleoblate.it*

FLO' LOUNGE BAR ☼ (U E6)

Live music, DJs, glamour, snacks buffet as well as a great view of the city. *Daily | Piazzale Michelangelo 84 | www.flofirenze. com*

LE MURATE (U E4)

Literary café, exhibition area, pizzeria, book shop and a stage: Florence finally has a public space for contemporary culture and it is in a beautifully restored former women's prison. *Daily | Piazza Madonna della Neve | www.lemurate. comune.fi.it*

NEGRONI FLORENCE BAR (U D5)

The drinks are a bit more expensive, but there is a free snacks buffet from 7pm–10pm: this formula seems to be working well, because all the new bars seem to be following the trend. *Daily | Via dei Renai 17 r | www.negronibar.com*

CAFFÈ SANT'AMBROGIO (U E4)

Very popular – every evening the guests spill out on to the square. *Daily | Piazza Sant'Ambrogio 7*

WHERE TO STAY

CASA HOWARD (U B3)

This guest house promises hip hospitality with, amongst other things, a room with a play corner for guests with children or one with a terrace for dog owners. *13 rooms | Via della Scala 18 | tel. 06 69 92 45 55 | www.casahoward.com | Expensive*

HOTEL CASCI (U C3)

Closing the cathedral square to traffic has had a very positive impact on the quality of this hotel. *24 rooms | Via Cavour 13 | tel. 0 55 21 16 86 | www.hotelcasci.com | Moderate*

HOTEL TORRE GUELFA (U C4)

The higher the tower, the more influential the family: this charming hotel boasts one of the last medieval towers in the city – it has the highest roof terrace! *16 rooms | Borgo Santi Apostoli 8 | tel. 05 52 39 63 38 | www.hoteltorreguelfa.com | Moderate– Expensive*

INFORMATION

(U B3) | Piazza della Stazione 4 | tel. 0 55 21 22 45; (U C3) | Via Cavour 1 r | tel. 0 55 29 08 32 | www.firenzeturismo.it

What a backdrop: the Roman amphitheatre in Fiesole

WHERE TO GO

CERTALDO (142 B3) (*∅ H9*)

The brick-paved main road leads straight through this medieval town (pop. 16,000) 45km/28mi south-west in the Elsa Valley, from the city gates Porta al Sole to the *Palazzo Pretorio*, where the coat of arms on the façade reveals who held the power here. In between is the *Palazzo Strozzi Ridolfi* with its atmospheric Renaissance courtyard and the *Casa Boccaccio* where the poet Giovanni Boccaccio – who caused quite a sensation with his 14th century novel 'Il Decamerone' (The Decameron) – spent the last years of his life. The upper town can be reached by funicular *(funicolare)* from the lower Piazza Boccaccia.

During July the old town becomes a stage for the INSIDER TIP week-long street theatre festival, *Mercantia di Certaldo*. It is also where you will find one of the best gourmet restaurants of the region, the *Osteria del Vicario (closed Wed | Via Rivellino 3 | tel. 05 71 66 82 28 | www.*

osteriadelvicario.it | Moderate–Expensive). Comfortable, ☆ rooms with views up to San Gimignano and a swimming pool are some of the features of *Relais Hotel Villa Tavolese* outside of town *(16 rooms | Marcialla | Via Tavolese 221 | tel. 05 71 66 02 24 | www.tavolese.com | Moderate)*.

FIESOLE (138 C5) (*∅ K7*)

The town (pop. 14,000) in the hills of Florence, which can be conveniently accessed with the bus line 7, was not always a suburb for well-to-do Florentines. Long before Florence came to power, the Etruscan settlement Faesulae flourished here. A steep hill from the central Piazza Mino da Fiesole leads up to the ☆ *San Francesco monastery* that dates back to 1399, which has a quaint mission museum *(daily 9.30am–noon and 3pm–5pm | admission free)*. The monastery garden leads down to the *San Romolo Cathedral* which dates back to the 11th century. Behind the cathedral is one of the hidden treasures of Tuscany, the *Museo Bandini (Wed–Mon 10am–7pm, winter 10am–4pm | 10 euros | Via Dupré 18)* full of sacred art and terracottas. The admission ticket can also be used for the *Archaeological Park (Wed–Mon 10am–7pm, winter 10am–4pm | Via Portigiani 1)* with its Roman theatre, thermal baths and temple. In front of the turnstile is the entrance to the *Caffè del Teatro Romano (summer daily 9.30am–8pm, longer during evening events)* where you can sit on the outside terrace and enjoy a cappuccino or a pasta against a lovely backdrop. The centrally located, friendly *Villa Sorriso (7 rooms | Via Gramsci 21 | tel. 05 55 90 27 | www.albergovillasorriso.net | Budget)* proves that in fine Fiesole, Tuscan hospitality need not be expensive. If you do not want to stay for the night: a walk across the ● *Via Vecchia Fiesolana*, will take you back to Florence in an hour, starting at the seminary. Between the stone walls, time seems to have stood still.

IMPRUNETA (142 C2) (*⌀ J8*)

In this town (pop. 15,000) south of Florence everything seems to be made from terracotta – even the postboxes! The building master Filippo Brunelleschi came here to source the bricks used to build Florence's cathedral. Today you can peek over artists' shoulders as they turn and fire the clay, amongst them *Mario Mariani (Via Lappello 29)*, who still works according to the traditional methods. Expect Tuscan flair, comfort, peace and quiet and a wonderful garden in the *Agriturismo Borgo de' Ricci. (6 apartments | Via Imprunetana per Pozzolatico 216/218 | Monte Oriolo | tel. 055 35 20 11 | www.borgodeiricci.com | Moderate)*.

LORO CIUFFENNA ⋊⋉
(143 F3) (*⌀ M9*)

This village (pop. 6000) sandwiched in the hills of the upper Arno valley, a good 50km/31mi south-east of Florence, is one of Italy's most beautiful. Among the build-

ings of historic interest are the Roman bridge that spans the Ciuffenna and the oldest flour mill in the area which is just below the bridge. Running through the town, is the bicycle-friendly, beautiful scenic road ⋊⋉ *Strada dei Sette Ponti*. During the Middle Ages some Romanesque churches built along the road. The most beautiful, the INSIDER**TIP** *Pieve San Pietro (daily 8am–noon and 3pm–5pm)* is in the hamlet of *Gropina* 2km/1.2mi south. It dates back to the 12th century and is decorated with traditional themes and motifs.

About 3km/1.8mi further, the *Osteria dell' Acquolina (closed Sun | Via Sette Ponti 26 | Terranuova Bracciolini | tel. 0 55 97 74 97 | Moderate)* serves local dishes made from seasonal ingredients – host Paolo Tizzanini is a supporter of the Slow Food movement. About 5km/3mi away, you can choose between the 28 villas, houses and luxury apartments of the Ferragamo family's *Borgo Il Borro (San Giustino Valdarno | tel. 0 55 97 70 53 | www.ilborro.it | Expensive)*.

MEDICI VILLAS ★ (138 B5) (*⌀ J7*)

A country estate with a garden for pleasure? The Medicis liked the idea so much that they had various splendid estates built around Florence between the 15th and the 17th century. The favourite was the *Villa Medicea (only by appointment tel. 05 54 27 97 55 | Viale Gaetano Pieraccini 17)* in *Careggi* (138 C5) (*⌀ J7*) which is on the northern edge of Florence, on the road towards Monte Morello. Designed by star architect Michelozzi, it is here that Cosimo I and Lorenzo the Magnificent surrounded themselves with artists and philosophers.

At the *Villa La Petraia (daily 8.15am–4.30pm, March–Oct longer, closed 2nd/3rd Mon | 2 euros | Via di Petraia 40)* in *Castello* (138 C5) (*⌀ J7*) about 6km/3.7mi in the direction of Sesto Fiorentino, you can view the magnificent garden in the Italian style. The towered, medieval castle was transformed by Bernardo Buontalenti in 1576. 17km/10mi west of Florence in *Poggio a Caiano* (138 A5) (*Ⓜ H7*) is one of the most beautiful villas, the ● *Villa Medicea (daily 8.15am–4.30pm, March–Oct longer, closed 2nd/3rd Mon | free admission | Piazza de' Medici 14)* which was commissioned by Lorenzo I in 1480. White and symmetrical with a curved side staircase and wide terraces, it was the model for later Renaissance villa architecture. Frescoes by Andrea del Sarto, Filippo Lippi and Jacopo da Pontormo decorate the villa's rooms.

MONTELUPO FIORENTINO
(142 B1) (*Ⓜ H8*)

The town (pop. 13,000, 30km/19mi west) owes its origins to the clay that it rests on and pottery, here pottery and ceramics production determines everyday life. This is documented in the Ceramics Museum *(Tue–Sat 10am–6pm | 5 euros | Piazza Vittorio Veneto 8 | www.museomontelupo. it)*. The entrance ticket is also valid for the *Archeological Museum (Tue–Sun 10am–6pm | Via Santa Lucia)* with displays of ceramic objects found in the area. In the ceramic outlet shop, *Bitossi (Via Castelucci 10)* you will find residual stock from their current production lines. On the outskirts of town you can overnight in style and comfort in the country hotel and wellness oasis, the *Borgo Sant'Ippolito (28 rooms | Via Chiantigiana 268 | Ginestra Fiorentina | tel. 05 58 71 34 23 | www.borgosantippo lito.it | Moderate)* housed in a meticulously restored monastery.

SAN CASCIANO IN VAL DI PESA
(142 BC21) (*Ⓜ J8–9*)

This town (pop. 15,000 and 20km/12mi south on the motorway to Siena) is famous for its Chianti wine and its magnificent setting. When driving here, it is best to take the road through Tavarnuzze and Sant'Andrea in Percussina, which starts

There are some interesting details on the façade of the Villa Medicea in Poggio a Caiano

at the motorway exit Firenze-Impruneta. The trip through the hills with vineyards and silvery shimmering olive groves is even more charming INSIDER TIP on a Vespa. Trips arranged by *Florence Town (Via de' Lamberti 1 | tel. 05 50 12 39 94 | www.florencetown.com).*

Tuscany is at its most beautiful along the old Etruscan road that runs via Mercatale to Panzano, where there are countless wine estates that have helped to write the history of Tuscan wine, such as the Corsini *Fattoria Le Corti (closed Mon | tel. 0 55 82 93 01 | www.principecorsini.com)* behind the town exit. The stretch between San Casciano via San Pancrazio to Tavarnelle Val di Pesa is also wonderful. In the small bar *Santa Cristina in Salivolpe* you can taste divine sheep's milk cheese from the nearby 😊 *Fattoria Corzano e Paterno (Via Paterno 10 | tel. 05 58 24 8179 | www.corzanoepaterno.it | Moderate).* The Swiss owners also rent out five comfortable apartments and three holiday homes.

VALDARNO (143 E–F 2–4) (*M L8–10*)

A local saying warns the inhabitants of the fertile Arno valley, between Florence and Arezzo, that 'every now and again the Arno returns home'. When it rains, the river swells with water from the mountains and turns into a raging torrent. Etruscans and Romans heeded the warning and built their settlements and roads in the hills. Their Via Cassia Vetus, the current Strada dei Sette Ponti, still winds through the same picture book landscape with its vineyards, olive groves, picturesque farmhouses, Romanesque churches and medieval villages. Here in *Regello* is the cosy and comfortable *Villa Rigacci. 28 rooms | Vaggio district 76 | tel. 05 58 65 67 18 | www.villarigacci.it | Moderate*

In the Middle Ages, Florence built its strategic outpost in the river's flood plains

and this lead to the development of some thriving towns, like *Montevarchi* and *Figline,* but they had to endure a number of destructive floods. Today the cathedrals of the modern age, i.e. outlet shops, are found here. *The Mall (daily 10am–7pm | Via Europa 8 | www.themall.it)* in *Leccio* has almost all the big fashion names under one roof. Prada fans need to go further south on the SS 69 past Montevarchi for the *Prada Outlet (Mon–Sat 10am–7pm, Sun 2pm–19pm | Levanella)* to spend their money.

VALLOMBROSA ☀☀ (143 F1) (*M L8*)

When it gets very hot during the summer, Florentines escape to the Pratomagno Mountains. In 1020 Giovanni Gualberto founded a hermitage 1000m/3281ft up in the shady valley 40km/29mi east of Florence. Eleven years later he founded the Vallombrosan Order and began construction of the abbey *(www.vallombrosa.it)*, today it is a fortress-like monastery. In the *monastery pharmacy (daily 10am–noon and 3pm–5pm)* you can purchase elixirs made by the monks. However the real star up here is the INSIDER TIP large old forest, on the way there, in *Donnini,* is the *Fattoria Montalbano (Via Montalbano 12 | tel. 05 58 65 21 58 | www.montalbano.it | Budget–Moderate)* offering eight holiday apartments and a wide variety of activities.

PISTOIA

(137 F4) (*M G–H6*) Vast forests and enchanting valleys filled with architectural evidence of a centuries-old history: this is the hinterland of the provincial capital on the southern slopes of the Tuscan-Emilian Apennines.

In the past, the industry here was based on iron ore processing, today however they rely on the production of furniture and textiles. The city itself (pop. 92,000) was founded by the Romans on the Via Cassia. In 1115 the market town gained independence and it enjoyed a brief period of prosperity. After its heyday it lived in the shadows of its mighty neighbours Pisa, Lucca and Florence. Almost the entire city centre around the vast cathedral square and the beautiful market square, the Piazza della Sala, is a pedestrian zone. Strolling through the city is a real pleasure, not least because the small specialist shops have not been ousted by branches of the large fashion labels.

The cathedral bell tower is a landmark in Pistoia

SIGHTSEEING

SAN ZENO CATHEDRAL ★

One of Tuscany's oldest churches (12th century) with a façade in the Romanesque style. The Crucifix Chapel contains the precious silver Saint James altar (1287–1456). Generations of silversmiths worked on the altar's 628 relief figures. The chunky Campanile (the 67m/220ft bell tower) cannot hide its initial purpose as a watchtower. *Daily 8am–9.30am, 10.30am–12.30pm and 3.30pm–7pm | 2 euros | Piazza del Duomo*

MUSEO MARINO MARINI

His recurring themes of horses, dancers and acrobats made this contemporary sculptor (1901–80) from Pistoia famous. *Mon–Sat 10am–6pm, winter 10am–5pm | 3.50 euros | Corso Fedi 30 | ww.fondazione marinomarini.it*

OSPEDALE DEL CEPPO

The hospital was founded in 1277 and was inspired by Brunelleschi's foundling hospital in Florence. The majolica frieze on the portico is a real gem – it dates from 1514 and was crafted in the workshop of Della Robbia and depicts the seven scenes of mercy mixed with scenes of the Virtues. *Via Matteotti 9*

SANT'ANDREA

Behind the two-tone façade of this Romanesque church is the most famous piece of art in the city, the first marble pulpit by Giovanni Pisano dating back to 1301. *Daily 8.30am–12.30pm and 3pm–6pm | Via Sant'Andrea*

FOOD & DRINK

TRATTORIA DELL'ABBONDANZA

The locals swear by the regional specialities like the vegetable soup, *farinata con verdure,* and the *fritto misto* made from chicken and rabbit. *Closed Thu afternoons and Wed | Via dell'Abbondanza 10 | tel. 05 73 36 80 37 | Moderate*

OSTERIA LA BOTTA GAIA

The lovely terrace with a view of the cathedral is one good reason to come here; another reason is their unusual interpretation of Tuscan dishes. *Closed Sun afternoon and Mon | Via del Lastrone 17 | tel. 05 73 36 56 02 | Moderate–Expensive*

CAFFÈ VALIANI ●

Enjoy your cappuccino in this former oratory, its walls and arches are decorated with ancient frescoes. *Daily 7am–10pm | Via Cavour 55*

SHOPPING

LA DOLCE PEONIA ↻

Confectioner Emanulea Regi experiments with organic ingredients in her bakery – try her delicious corn and blueberry biscuits! *Viale Petrocchi 122*

ENTERTAINMENT

WINE BAR CAPATOSTA

A great place for a glass of wine, on the Piazza della Sala, where young and old meet at twilight. *Daily from 7pm | Piazza della Sala 1*

WHERE TO STAY

HOTEL LEON BIANCO

A simple three-star hotel that is peaceful, affordable and centrally located. *30 rooms | Via Panciatichi 2 | tel. 057 32 66 75 | www.hotelleonbianco.it | Budget*

VILLA DE' FIORI

In this hotel, right in front of the city gates in the old town, you get the feeling that you are visiting your favourite relatives. Comfortable rooms, lush gardens, good food and massages round off this feel-good experience. *6 rooms, 2 apartments | Via di Biginao e Castel Bovani 39 | tel. 05 73 45 03 51 | www.villadefiori.it | Moderate*

INFORMATION

Piazza Duomo 4 | tel. 0 57 32 16 22 | www.pistoia.turismo.toscana.it

WHERE TO GO

INSIDER TIP ABETONE
(137 D2) (∅ F5)

This may be a real surprise to many: Tuscany has a substantial ski resort area in the Apennines. Some 1900m/6232ft high, it covers four majestic valleys, with modern facilities and 50km/31mi of well maintained ski slopes with varying levels of difficulty *(www.abetone.it)*. All the usual magic of mountain huts and après ski, for instance in the disco bar *Lupo Bianco (summer Fri–Wed 7am–8pm, winter daily 7am–1am | Piazza Abetone)*. The main centre is 45km/28mi to the north in the high altitude village of *Abetone* with its piazza with two stone pyramids. During the summer hiking enthusiasts come here to hike in the mountains. Simple, comfortable accommodation, with a view of the Monte Libro Aperto, can be found at the family hotel *Primula (16 rooms | Via Brennero 195 | tel. 0 57 36 01 08 | www.hotelprimula.com | Budget)*.

INSIDER TIP FATTORIA LE CELLE ●
(138 A4) (∅ H6)

The owner, Guiliano Gori, has been inviting high-profile artists here since 1982. The artists create their artworks on site and the landscaped garden (8km/5mi east of Pistoia in Santomato) now has over 60 sculptures and installations. Free viewing during summer but only by appointment. *Via Montalese 7 | tel. 05 73 47 94 86 | www. goricoll.it*

MONTAGNA PISTOIESE
(137 E–F3) *(ဖြ G6)*

Secluded lakes, wild mountain streams, fortified stone villages and ancient streets attract nature lovers in the vast beech and chestnut forests of the Pistoia Mountains. Hikers who love culture can also enjoy the themed routes that take you through the hidden evidence of the past. Information is distributed at various locations ☺ *Ecomuseo della Montagna Pistoiese (tel. 0 57 39 74 61 | www.provincia.pistoia. it/ecomuseo).* Accommodation is in the suitably rustic *Agriturismo Il Gufo (4 apartments | Via Porta Viti 34 | tel. 34 70 59 91 59 | www.gufotuscany.com | Budget– Moderate)* at *San Marcello Pistoiese,* ideal for day trips out in nature and art. If you prefer to lounge around, you can enjoy the stunning mountain scenery from the edge of the swimming pool.

MONTECATINI TERME ★
(137 E4) *(ဖြ G7)*

A mixture of minerals, enriched with essential elements and salts over the course of millions of years: this is the secret of the healing waters of Montecatini Terme. Ever popular through the ages – even the Romans came here to be cured of liver ailments and rheumatism – celebrities like Guiseppe Verdi, the Shah of Persia and Gary Cooper have sipped on its warm healing waters. At the end of the 18th century the Tuscan Duke Pietro Leopoldo I, created the spa around the thermal springs. Amongst others, he built the classical *Terme Leopoldine* and the glamorous ● *Stabilimento Tettuccio* with its magnificent column porticos and water fountains with marble counters.

Apart from this, the image of the resort town (pop. 21,000) which lies a good 15km/9mi west of Pistoia, is dominated by its art nouveau architecture. North-east of the spa, a red funicular takes you up to the protected Montecatini Alto. If you want to spoil yourself you will be in good hands in the *Grand Hotel & La Pace (130 rooms | Via della Toretta 1 | tel. 05 72 92 40 | www.grandhotellapace.it | Expensive)*, the oldest hotel in the town.

The region around Montecatini is also a favourite destination for gourmets, especially because a ● INSIDER TIP master chocolatier *(Slitti | Via Francesca 1268 | www.slitti.it)* is at work in the neighbouring village *Monsummano Terme.* A bit further to the south-east, through the magnificent Tuscan landscape, is *Lamporecchio* and the ecologically-run wine and olive estate ● ☺ *Balduccio (Via Greppiano 31 | www.balduccio.it)* where you can sample the local produce.

PESCIA
(137 D4) *(ဖြ F6–7)*

Just 25km/15.5mi west of Pistoia is the little town (pop. 20,000) of Pescia, famous for its beautiful flowers. The colourful flowers are sold early in the morning at the *Mercato dei Fiori* at the train station. A river, the Pescia, divides the medieval centre of the town in two parts. On the western shore lies the older, secular part. Its centre is the long *Piazza Mazzini,* one of the most beautiful squares in Tuscany. The eastern shore is the religious centre. Its treasure lies in the *San Franceso* church – an altarpiece by Bonaventura Berlinghieri (1235). The wonderfully situated wine estate, *Marzalla (Via Collecchio 1 | tel. 05 72 49 07 51 | www.marzalla.it | Expensive)* with its seven apartments, garden and restaurant is the ideal base to set out for tours into the Nievole valley and the surrounding mountains.

Leonardo's ingenious machines and devices are displayed in the Vinci museum

SAN MINIATO ★ (141 E–F2) (*⑭ G8*)

The tower that looks out over the town (pop. 28,000) 40km/25mi south of Pistoia, dates back to the time when the place was an important administrative centre for the Holy Roman Empire. For this reason Frederick II built his *Rocca Federiciana* here in 1218. Only the tower managed to withstand the test of time but it was destroyed, along with the whole town, by German troops in 1944 before being rebuilt again in 1957. Today San Miniato enjoys world fame as the city of the white truffle.

The 129 steps up to the top of the ☆ tower (Tue–Sun 10am–5pm | 3.50 euros) are worth the effort because the view over the Arno plateau is fantastic. Just below it is the 13th century cathedral and alongside it a staircase that leads to the *Piazza della Republica*. During November, the square plays host to a truffle fair.

If you wish to try local game specialities or truffle dishes in a rustic atmosphere, the *Taverna dell'Ozio (closed Mon | Via Zara 85 | tel. 05 71 46 28 62 | Moderate)* is the right place. Reservations recommended! The rooms ☆ in the hotel *Albergo Miravalle (21 rooms | Piazzetta del Castello 3 | tel. 05 71 41 80 75 | www.albergomiravalle.com | Moderate)* will surprise you – either with a four poster bed or a wonderful view.

VINCI (137 F5–6) (*⑭ G–H7*)

This town, (pop. 14,000) between Pistoia and Empoli, is dominated by Leonardo da Vinci, who was born out of wedlock here in 1452. Two museums are dedicated to him. The more interesting one is the *Museo Leonardiano (daily 9.30am–7pm, winter 9.30am–6pm | 7 euros | Piazza dei Guidi | www.museoleonardiano.it)* in the castle of Conti Guidi. Here they do not concentrate on Leonardo the artist, but on Leonardo the scientist and inventor. A footpath leads 3km/1.8mi north to his birthplace in the town district of *Anchiano, (daily 9.30am–7pm, winter 9.30am–6pm | free admission)*. The path through the olive groves, forests and vineyards is much more attractive than the building.

Donatello and Michelozzi's joint
venture: the Santo Stefano pulpit

PRATO

(138 B4–5) *(∅ H–J7)* **Art tourists normally avoid this 'Manchester of Italy' with its industrial belt and anonymous suburban architecture.**

Since the 14th century Tuscany's second largest city (pop. 190,000) has been spinning, weaving and exporting quality yarn and this is where the large Italian labels have their alta moda made. Many sewing factories are now in Chinese hands though, which explains the Chinatown outside the well-preserved medieval city wall.

What many do not know is that Prato has a very beautiful town centre filled with art treasures and attractive religious and secular buildings – the results of centuries of symbioses between economy and art. The large pedestrian zone is also the per-

fect shopping area, especially for all things to do with fashionable textiles. You can get there by train or bus and the train station is right in the centre.

SIGHTSEEING

CASTELLO DELL'IMPERATORE
The massive castle with towers and high crenellated walls was supposedly built for the 13th century Emperor Frederic II as a stronghold on the way to his home in southern Italy. He did not live to see the castle's completion. *Mon–Fri 4pm–7pm, Sat/Sun 10am–1pm and 4pm–7pm | free admission | Piazza Santa Maria delle Carceri*

CENTRO PER L'ARTE CONTEMPORANEA LUIGI PECCI
One of the oldest museums for contemporary art in Italy is again making name for itself with high-profile temporary exhibitions by artists from all over the world. This centre for contemporary art, which is situated 2km/1.2mi south of the city centre, is also the starting point for organised tours that trail through the city, for example, to Henry Moore's marble sculpture on the Piazza San Marco, or the sculpture park of Fattioria Le Celle. During the summer it is often open in the evenings for concerts. *Wed–Mon 10am–7pm | 5 euros | Viale della Repubblica 277 | www.centropecci.it*

SANTO STEFANO CATHEDRAL ★
Here the external pulpit on the corner immediately draws your attention. The *Sacro Cingolo*, a gold threaded wool belt said to work miracles, is displayed here several times a year. The pulpit was made by Michelozzi, the balustrade with cherub reliefs by Donatello. The green and white striped marble façade was added to the cathedral in 1386 and almost a century later, the glazed terracotta lunette by Andrea della Robbia. In the impressive

interior Filippo Lippi, a son of the city, painted two series of frescoes on the walls of the main choir chancel: on the left the life of the church patron and on the right that of John the Baptist. *Daily 7am–7pm (choir chancel Mon–Sat 10am–5pm, Sun 3pm–5pm) | 3 euros | Piazza del Duomo*

INSIDER TIP ► MUSEO DEL TESSUTO ●

Underneath the vaults of a former textile factory, the history of Prato's textile industry is documented with machines, production techniques and priceless fabrics from bygone centuries. Special displays complement the current collection. *Mon–Fri 10am–6pm, Sat 10am–2pm, Sun 4pm–7pm | 6 euros | Via Santa Chiara 24 | www.museodeltessuto.it*

PALAZZO PRETORIO

One look at the fortress-like palace on the Piazza Comunale will tell you that it has been constantly changed over the centuries. It was built in 1284 as the seat of the city's bailiff and today is one of the most impressive palaces in central Italy. The monument in front of the palace commemorates Prato's textile merchant, Francesco di Marco Datini (1335–1410), a great philanthropist. The loggias on the ground floor have been walled up, so you enter the palace via a staircase on the first floor. Due to renovations the art collection that is usually displayed here – with works by Filippo Lippi and the like – is currently being exhibited in the cloister of San Domenico. *Sun–Thu 9am–1pm, Fri/Sat 9am–1pm and 3pm–6pm | 4 euros | Piazza San Domenico*

FOOD & DRINK

ENOTECA BARNI

This restaurant has two faces: in the afternoon it is a cantina for bankers and business people and at night it becomes an elegant restaurant serving creative Tuscan cuisine. *Closed Sun | Via Ferrucci 22 | tel. 05 74 60 78 45 | Moderate*

RAZMATAZ

You might just be lucky enough to have John Malkovich at the table next to you, working on his new menswear collection. Excellent starters! *Closed Mon | Piazza Mercatale 110 | tel. 05 74 44 86 19 | Moderate*

ECO-MUSEUMS

How can the rural population best illustrate their relationship to their natural environment, one that clearly shapes their local identity? In the Pistoia Mountains and in the Casentino the answer is eco-museums. This is not your usual cultural showcase, where the cultural and artistic highlights of the area are represented. Rather it is an innovative cultural project with multiple sites that each address different aspects of the local industrial culture – crafts, life-style, narrative tradition. This is only possible because the local residents take an active and voluntary responsibility for their own culture, environment and tradition. In the Pistoia Mountains *(www.provincia.pistoia.it/ecomuseo)* visitors are shown how ice was preserved or how iron was produced using hydropower. In Casentino *(www.casentino.toscana.it/ecomuseo)* a coal maker explains how charcoal was produced, or millwrights explain how the old watermills work.

SHOPPING

BISCOTTIFICIO ANTONIO MATTEI

The city's famous almond biscotti biscuits, *cantuccini di Prato,* are baked here according to the original recipe. *Mon closed | Via Ricasoli 20/22 | www.antoniomattei.it*

INSIDER TIP OPIFICIOJM

John Malkovich's concept store is a showcase for local creatives, designers and artisans and promotes Tuscan culture and lifestyle. The wine and specialities in the integrated ItaliaBar are also guaranteed to be 'Made in Tuscany'. *Mon 10am–7.30pm, Tue–Sat 10am–midnight, Sun 6pm–midnight | Piazza San Marco 39 | www.opificiojm.it*

ENTERTAINMENT

CAFFÈ AL TEATRO

Tapas, drinks and live music almost every evening. *Closed Sun | Via Verdi 28 | www.caffealteatro.net*

KING'S PUB

Nice pub with decent prices, especially popular with the younger crowd. *Closed Wed | Via Garibaldi 148*

WHERE TO STAY

ALBERGO GIARDINO

Centrally located, clean rooms, private garage: all good reasons to choose this friendly hotel. *28 rooms | Via Magnolfi 2–6 | tel. 05 74 60 65 88 | www.giardinohotel.com | Budget*

VILLA RUCELLAI

Unpretentious rooms with a lot of character await you in this Renaissance villa 4km/2.5mi outside the city gates. *11 rooms | Via di Canneto 16 | tel. 05 74 46 03 92 | www.villarucellai.it | Moderate*

INFORMATION

Piazza Duomo 8 | tel. 0 57 42 41 12 | www.pratoturismo.it

WHERE TO GO

MUGELLO

(138–139 C–D 2–4) (*ØD J–L 5–6*)

Gently rolling hills? Nothing of the sort! Behind Prato, Tuscany has a wild side where massive forests stretch out in the valleys south of the Tuscan Emilian Apennines, home to hermitages, isolated and abandoned villages, splendid villas, waterfalls and, more recently, even wolves. The region has for some time been popular with adventure and outdoor enthusiasts who prefer to explore its nature on foot, by bicycle or on horseback along its well signed-posted hiking trails. Excellent information material is available at the tourism office *Comunità Montana (Via Togliatti 45 | tel. 0 55 84 52 71 85 | www.mugellotoscana.it)* in *Borgo San Lorenzo.*

Those coming from Prato via the A 1 will find the exit to Barberino di Mugello and the *Barberino Designer Outlet Village (Via Meucci | www.outlet-village.it/barberino),* where all the big names in the fashion world are represented. From there it is a stone's throw to the *Lago di Bilancino* reservoir popular with windsurfers, sailors and sunbathers. Two establishments rent out umbrellas and also provide bar and restaurant facilities and create a party atmosphere in the evening.

One of the most beautiful villas in Tuscany, *Villa Le Maschere (65 rooms | Via Nazionale 75 | tel. 055 84 74 32 | www.villalemaschere.it | Expensive)* in *Barberino* is where you can enjoy all the amenities of a luxury hotel, while the *Agriturismo Sanvitale (8 rooms | Via Campagna 20 | tel. 05 58 40 11 58 | www.agriturismosanvitale.it | Budget–Moderate)* 20km/12mi east in

Luco di Mugello, is more down-to-earth and will give you a good feeling of the country, the people and the way of life. On your way there you will pass the *Autodromo del Mugello (www.mugellocircuit. it)* racing circuit where motorcycle and Formula-1 events are regularly held. As a contrast to this there is the **INSIDER TIP** nature reserve around the 1000 year old *Badia di Moscheta* 17km/10.5mi north on the road to Firenzuola. Visitors come for the delicious Tuscan steak dish, *bistecca fiorentina* serverd in the restaurant *Badia di Moscheta. Closed Mon/Tue | Via di Moscheta 898 | tel. 05 58 14 43 05 | Budget–Moderate)*

SCARPERIA (139 D3) (*ш K6*)

Does the elegant *Palazzo Vicario* in the Tuscan city of knives (pop. 7800) some 45km/28mi north-east of Prato seem familiar? That is because this is a smaller version of the Palazzo Vecchio in Florence. The interior is strictly medieval, only the artrium is painted and decorated with coats of arms. To the left you can go to the knife musem *Museo dei Ferri Taglienti (summer Mon–Fri 3.30pm–7.30pm, Sat/ Sun 10am–1pm and 3.30–7.30pm, otherwise Sat/Sun 10am–1pm and 3–6.30pm | 3 euros).* Wide variety of handcrafted knives to suit every budget *Coltellerie Berti (Via Roma 43 | www.coltellerieberti.it).*

VICCHIO
(139 D4) (*ш L6*)

This town (pop. 7000 and 55km/34mi east of Prato) is a place of pilgrimage for art lovers as it was here, in the green hills of the Sieve valley, that both Giotto (1267–1337) and Beato Angelico (1387–1455) were born. A sign on the northern town border shows the way to *Giotto's birthplace (summer Thu 10am–1pm and 3pm–7pm, winter Sat/Sun 10am–1pm | 4 euros | Vespignano district)* where a multimedia display details the life and work of the artist. While in the vicinity, you should stop at the *Casa del Prosciutto (closed Mon/ Tue | Via del Ponte 1 | tel. 0 55 84 40 31 | Moderate),* a mixture of grocery store and an osteria, on the old bridge towards Barbania. More culinary souvenirs – chestnut products, sheep's milk cheeses and potato-filled tortelli – are all available from the agricultural cooperative ⊙ *Il Forteto (closed Mon/Tue | www.forteto.it)* 5km/3mi towards Pontassieve.

Another side of Tuscany: the nature reserves in Mugello around the Lago di Bilancino

AREZZO, SIENA & CHIANTI

Arezzo, the golden and Siena, the beautiful: both provincial capitals in the south-east of the region seem to try and outdo each other with their art treasures. And even their scenic landscapes – the hills around Siena and the plateaus of Arezzo, which rise up to the Apennine mountains – are characterised by great culture and magnificent nature.

AREZZO

(144 C4) (*ØJ N10*) Arezzo is one of Italy's oldest cities (pop. 100,000) and it has always been synonymous with great art,

WHERE TO START?
It is not easy to find a parking space but the best bet is at the **Piazza del Popolo**, right near to the Basilica San Francesco with its famous frescoes. A more relaxing option is to travel there by train – it is only a ten minute walk from the train station. From here you can go via the boulevard Corso Italaie, with its elegant shops and little alleys, to the impressive Santa Maria della Pieve church and the centre of Arezzo, the Piazza Grande.

Castles, churches, cloisters and many curves: the Middle Ages dominate throughout Casentino and the Orcia valley

elegant craftmanship and valuable antiques. Nevertheless this former Etruscan city, which is located at a strategic intersection of the fertile Chianti valley and the mountainous region of Casentino, only shows its true colours when you take a closer look.

First you have to overlook Arezzos anonymous, sprawling and overdeveloped pheriphery – but behind it, the city is a thriving provincial centre, with an historic old town that delights with its magnificent palaces, charming squares, elegant shops and wonderful atmosphere.

The centre, which runs up a steep slope, is small enough to easily explore on foot. There are cheap combination tickets available at all the museums for the most important attractions.

SIGHTSEEING

CASA VASARI

This magnificent house is one of the few preserved artist homes of the Renaissance: built and occupied by painter and architect Giorgio Vasarie (1511–1574). He is responsible for the Uffizi Gallery in Florence and his artist biographies helped create stand-

MUSEO ARCHEOLOGICO NAZIONALE GAIO CILNIO MECENATE

The largest Estruscan art treasure, the Chimera of Arezzo, is now in a museum in Florence. Nevertheless, you should not miss out on the displays in this former 16th century monastery which was built over a Roman amphitheatre. *Daily 8.30am– 7.30pm | 4 euros | Via Margaritone 10*

It took Piero della Francesca a decade to paint the frescoes in the choir of San Francesco

ard works of art history. *Mon and Wed–Sat 8am–7pm, Sun 8.30am–1pm | 2 euros | Via XX Settembre 55*

SAN PIETRO MAGGIORE CATHEDRAL

One remarkable feature of this 13th century Gothic building are the stained glass windows by Guillaume de Marcillat (16th century) but it also has another great art treasure, a small fresco of Mary Magdalene by Piero della Francesca in the left aisle. The cathedral is next to the city park, the Passeggio del Prato. *Daily 7.30am–12.30pm and 3pm–6.30pm | Piazza Duomo*

MUSEO STATALE D'ARTE MEDIEVALE E MODERNA

The most beautiful museum in the city is this one in a 15th century Renaissance palace. The exhibition includes sandstone sculptures from the 8th century and the most expansive majolica pottery collection in Tuscany. *Tue–Sun 8.30am–7pm | 4 euros | Via San Lorentino 8*

PIAZZA GRANDE ★

Does this asymetric, slightly sloping square seem familiar? You may well recognise it from the film set of Roberto Begnini's 'La vita è bella' (Life is Beautiful). This square, which was designed as a market place, has been used as backdrop venue for events like the medieval knight's tournament, Giostra del Saracino, which was first held here in 1593. For a box seat from which to watch the hustle and bustle, find yourself a café table under the beautiful Loggia del Vasari (1537) or on the steps of the courthouse and the elegant Palazzo Fraternità dei Laici on the western side. The narrow town houses date back to the Middle Ages.

SAN FRANCESCO
Behind the unadorned façade of this Gothic basilica is a major work from the early Renaissance. A ten piece ⭐ fresco by Piero della Francesca, the 'Legend of the Holy Cross'. After a lengthy restoration it is now quite luminous and back to its former glory. The artist worked for more than a decade on the 3230ft² narrative, bringing to life the history of the Holy Land and setting it in his own Tuscany. Arezzo becomes Jerusalem, the Tuscan landscape becomes the biblical realm and the Queen of Sheba becomes a Renaissance noble-woman. *Summer Mon–Fri 9am–6.30pm, Sat 9am–6pm, Sun 1pm–6pm, winter Mon–Fri 9am–5.30pm, Sat 9am–5pm, Sun 1pm–5pm, admission only with advance reservation tel. 05 75 35 27 27 or www.apt. arezzo.it. Tickets collected from the tourism office next door | 6 euros | Piazza San Francesco 1*

SANTA MARIA DELLA PIEVE
A church that is a favourite with the locals, its lovely choir apse faces the Piazza Grande and its front, with its impressive combination of columns and arches from the 12th century, makes it one of the most beautiful Romanesque monuments in Tuscany. The bell tower is known locally as the 'tower with a hundred holes' because of its 40 Romanesque twin windows. *Daily 9am–noon and 3pm–6pm | Corso Italia 7*

FOOD & DRINK

ANTICA OSTERIA L'AGANIA
Family-owned restaurant serving classic Tuscan dishes and seasonal specialities.

MARCO POLO HIGHLIGHTS

Village centre and market place: the medieval Piazza Grande in Arezzo

Closed Mon | V. Mazzini 10 | tel. 05 75 29 53 81 | www.agania.com | Budget–Moderate

LOGGE VASARI

Choose a table underneath the arcade with a view over the Piazza Grande – but do not forget to eat whilst taking in the spectacle as it would be a pity to miss out on the excellent food! *Closed Tue| Piazza Grande 19 | tel. 0575295894 | www.logge vasari.it | Moderate–Expensive*

SHOPPING

BUSATTI

Fine bedding and table linen in the Tuscan style and colours. *Corso Italia 48 | www. busatti.com*

MERCATO DELL'ANTIQUARIATO

Every first weekend of the month the Piazza Grande is transformed into the biggest antiques shop in Italy.

ENTERTAINMENT

MARTINI POINT

The street bar guarantees action long after 9pm. *Daily | Corso Italia 285*

ROCK 'N' ROLL

First you eat your fill then you burn off the calories you consumed! Closed Mon | *Via Calamandrei 183 | www.rocknrollclub.it*

WHERE TO STAY

HOTEL PATIO

Bruce Chatwin's travel stories inspired the creation of this peaceful city hotel in an old city palace. *7 rooms | Via Cavour 23 | tel. 05 75 40 19 62 | www.hotelpatio.it | Expensive*

VILLA I BOSSI

Four-poster beds, splendid salons and trimmed box hedges in the baroque garden all make this country villa a dream destination. Located at the city gates. *17 rooms | district Gragnone 44 | tel. 05 75 36 56 42 | www.villaibossi.com | Moderate*

INFORMATION

Piazza della Repubblica 28 | tel. 05 75 37 76 78 | www.apt.arezzo.it

WHERE TO GO

ANGHIARI (145 D4) (*ⓜ O9*)

Just before Sansepolcro, the dead-straight *stradone* SP 43 provincial road leads to this proud village with its beautiful old town (pop. 5800). The town has numerous workshops and craftsmen including the headquarters of the linen weavers *Busatti (Via Mazzini 14)*. Most of the streets off the car park lead into the town's medieval labyrinth of steep stairways, alleyways and arches and – rising above the its houses, *palazzi* and squares – the city hall bedecked in various coats of arms.

In case you want to stay longer, the rustic *Agriturismo Il Sasso (2 rooms, 2 apartments | district San Lorenzo 38 | tel. 05 75 78 70 78 | www.agriturismoilsasso.it | Budget–Moderate)* 3km/18mi out of town is a good choice. The owner will gladly organise cultural trips and other activities.

CAMALDOLI (144 B1) (*ⓜ N7*)

This village founded in 1024 by Saint Romuald is characterised by magnificent scenery and wonderful tranquillity. The Camaldolese monastery *(Monastero)* and hermitage *(Eremo)* 45km/28mi to the north is a destination for trips as well as a retreat for people who are searching for contemplation. There is the massive monastery (825m/2706ft) with its beautiful cloister as well as the monastery pharmacy. The hermitage is hidden a further 3km/1.8mi into the forest. There are still

monks living in its 20 cells so you can only visit the cell that belonged to the order's founder, the church and the chapter house *(monastery and hermitage Mon–Sat 9am–noon and 3pm–6pm, winter until 5pm | www.camaldoli.it)*. The 13 rooms in the *Locanda dei Baroni (Via di Camaldoli 5 | tel. 05 75 55 60 15 | www.alberghicamaldoli.it | Budget)* are rather monastic but the food in the restaurant is good and affordable.

CASENTINO
(144 B–C 1–2) (*ⓜ M–O 6–8*)

The secluded valley in the north of Arezzo, with the Pratomagno in the west and the Alpe di Catenaia in the east, is a world of its own. During the Middle Ages the massive mountain forests were retreats for monks and later for rich patricians who built their summer residences here. In 1990 a large area of the countryside, 135 square miles, was declared a national park and nowadays there are even wolves once again roaming amongst the trees. You can explore the 600km/373mi long network of paths on foot, horse or bicycle. Information and maps are available in the visitors centre of the *Parco Nazionale delle Foreste Casentinesi* in *Pratovechio (Via Brocchi 7 | tel. 0 57 55 03 01 | www.parcoforestecasentinesi.com)*.

The administrative centre is the lively *Bibbiena* (pop. 10,000) with its beautiful old town. The winding SP 208 takes you in an easterly direction up the 🔅● *Abbazia La Verna (www.santuariolaverna.org)* 1128m/3700 ft. You need not be a pilgrim to stay in the very affordable *sanctuary (Chiusi della Verna | tel. 05 75 53 42 10 | www.santuariolaverna.org, keyword accoglienza | Budget)*. The monastery is situated on a precipice in the midst of beech and spruce trees and was founded by Saint Francis of Assisi. It is here where his stigmata manifested itself in 1224. This stone-grey complex has a rather unfriendly exterior but

Narrow alleyways and steep, cobbled steps characterise Cortona

its interior is a labyrinth assemblage of chapels, churches, monk's cells and the cave where St Francis would retreat to for prayer.

Along the road from Bibbiena to La Verna lies the hotel-style *Agriturismo La Collina delle Stelle (9 rooms, 2 apartments | district Casanova 63 | tel. 05 75 59 48 06 | www. lacollinadellestelle.it | Budget–Moderate)*, a good starting point for expeditions into the surrounding area.

CORTONA ★
(144–145 C–D6) *(Ⓜ O12)*

Churches, monasteries and palaces crowd together between weathered stone walls, steep narrow alleys and cobbled stairs that lead to attractive little squares. Cortona is an old Etruscan town (pop. 23,000)

that is exactly as the Tuscany of your imagination. The same could be said about the elegant guest house *Il Falconiere (19 rooms | district San Martino 370 | tel. 05 75 61 26 79 | www.ilfalconiere.com | Expensive)*, where there is also a master chef in the kitchen.

This wonderful town begs to be explored and it is best done so on foot, wearing comfortable shoes. The climb up the Via Guelfa from the car park below the city wall is tedious but as soon as you arrive at the *Piazza della Repubblica* you will instantly forget about the hike. The square between the 14th century town hall above the large flight of stairs and the Palazzo del Popolo, with its 13th century open arches, is a stage on which everyday life unfolds (especially during the classical music festival in mid July, *www.festivaldelsole.com*). Street cafés invite you in, shops offer culinary delights and craft work, and in the Museum for Archaeology and City History *MAEC (April–Oct daily 10am–7pm, Nov–March Tue–Sun 10am–5pm | 8 euros | Piazza Signorelli 9 | www.cortonamaec.org)* you can admire the curious collections of ancient artefacts. Afterwards its over to the 11th century cathedral and its ☀ viewing platform. Opposite, in the inconspicuous *Museo Diocesano (April–Sept daily Oct Tue–Sun 10am–7pm, Nov–March Tue–Sun 10am–5pm | 5 euros | Piazza del Duomo 1 | www.cortona-musei.it)* is one of the most famous paintings in the world, the 'Annunciation' by Beato Angelico.

On your way back to the car, you will pass the *De Gustibus (daily 9.30am–8pm, in winter closed Tue/Wed | Via Guelfa 73 | tel. 05 75 61 37 31 | Budget–Moderate)* which serves panini and local specialities.

LUCIGNANO (144 B6) *(Ⓜ M12)*

You can hardly find a more vivid example of a medieval castle village on a hill. When walking through this village (pop. 3600 and 30km/18.5mi south-west) you understand how a settlement can develop within a fortress. The village is dominated by the impressive 16th century collegiate church, *San Michele Arcangelo*. The *Palazzo Pretorio*, decorated with crests and coats of arms, behind the church to the left is almost 300 years older. Stepping through the southern city gate *Porta San Giusti* is like making a trip to the Middle Ages and back.

POPPI (144 B2) (*M–N8*)

The 12th century medieval castle of Count Guidi is seen as one of the best preserved monuments of Tuscany. It is situated 40km/25mi north of Arezzo and dominates the village (pop. 6400) and surrounding area. At Ponte a Poppi you turn left over an old stone bridge and go up a forested hill.

At the junction is the *Osteria del Tempo Perso (Via Roma 79)* where they serve the best *panini* in the area. Walking through the castle's courtyard *(March–Oct daily 10am–6pm, Nov–Feb Thu–Sun 10am–5pm | 4 euros | www.castellodipoppi.it)*, decorated with coats of arms, a curved staircase takes you into the living rooms. The chapel is quite beautiful, it has 14th century frescoes and there is a library with valuable manuscripts. Take some time to stroll across the *Via Cavour* lined with arches, to the Romanesque abbey church *San Fedele*.

SANSEPOLCRO (145 E3) (*P9*)

The birthplace of Piero Della Francesca (see Trips & Tours) is situated 35km/21.5mi east in the middle of a landscape of rolling hills sloping up to distant mountains. Inside the medieval city walls (pop. 16,500) there is the atmosphere of a rural village. The bronze monument, close to the gigantic 1591 loggia, reveals that the village has a long tradition of lace making.

The Boninsegni family have converted the manor house on their estate into holiday accommodation *(Agriturismo La Conca | 13 rooms and apartments | district Paradiso 16 | tel. 05 75 73 33 01 | www.laconca.it | Moderate)* with a relaxed and friendly atmosphere. In the tourism office *(Via Matteotti 8 | tel. 05 75 74 05 36 | www.apt. arezzo.it)* you can get information about the various themed walks, such as the one that follows in the footsteps of Francis of Assisi *(www.sentierodifrancesco.it)*.

STIA (144 A1) (*M7*)

Nature lovers know this pretty little village (40km/25mi north of Arezzo on the slopes of Monte Falterone) because it is the source

LOW BUDGET

▶ Arezzo, the city of gold, naturally also has a jewellery outlet: *Unoaerre | Via Fiorentina 550 | www.unoaerre.it*

▶ The term *vino sfuso* means 'on tap' and many wine estates and shops sell wine this way. Even Chianti Classico or Rosso di Montalcino can be bought for less than half the bottle price. You only need an empty 5 litre bottle which can then be refilled again. Warning: *vino sfuso* is not wine that travels well.

▶ 75 euros for an en suite double room with breakfast in Siena? This is possible in the converted women's convent *Alma Domus (28 rooms | Via Camporegio 37 | tel. 0 57 74 41 77 | www.hotelalmadomus.it)*. With a little luck, you might even get a ✷ room with a panoramic view of the old town.

of the Arno, blacksmiths because their world championships take place here every two years and fashion lovers for its panno di lana, a brightly coloured Tuscan fabric. Nestled in dense forests, this village (pop. 3000) also impresses with its long *Piazza Tanucci* and colourful houses, some of them with arcades. There is also the hotel and restaurant, *Falterona (15 rooms | Piazza Tanucci 85 | tel. 05 75 50 45 69 | www.albergofalterona.it | Budget)* serving regional cuisine and the showroom for the wool cooperative TACS *(www.tacs.it),* which has their outlet in the *Via Sanarelli 49.*

On the way to Arezzo, on the right side above Pratovecchio, is the 12th century INSIDER TIP *Pieve San Pietro di Romena*, one of the most beautiful Romanesque churches in this part of Tuscany.

SIENA

MAP ON PAGE 62
(143 D6) (*ØØ K11*) **This majestic city (pop. 55,000) is an Italian marvel. Set high in glorious hill terrain and protected by fortified walls, and it has managed to retain its medieval character right into the modern age. Strict building regulations have ensured that nothing disturbs the harmony of the cityscape. Even cars and television aerials are banned from its centre.**

During the Middle Ages this city republic, which is spread over three hills, developed into the most important trade and financial centre in the area and that didn't change even after they were subjugated by Florence in 1555. The Sienese sense of loyalty and belonging to their city is very pronounced, especially during the Palio *(www.ilpalio.org)* when the famous (and controversial) horse races take place every year on 2 July and 16 August. Ten of the 17 districts, or *contrade*, of Siena compete against each other. The horses race around the Piazza del Campo three times and the winning *contrada* carry the standard or the *palio*.

Before the city walls you will find the metered parking area *(www.sienaparcheggi. com)* but the bus is a far better option as it goes to the Via di Città which in turn leads to the Piazza del Campo.

SIGHTSEEING

INSIDER TIP COMPLESSO MUSEALE SANTA MARIA DELLA SCALA

Almost 1000 years ago the Museum for Archaeology was a place where pilgrims on their way to Rome stayed overnight under fresco-decorated vaults and later the sick, poor and orphans were cared for. Today it is home to museums for archaeology, contemporary art and children. *Daily 10.30am–6.30pm, in winter until 4.30pm | 6 euros | Piazza Duomo 2 | www.santamariadellascala.com*

SANTA MARIA CATHEDRAL

The foundation stone for this spectacular cathedral, with its light and dark striped façade by Giovanni Pisano, was laid in 1136 and was only completed 200 years later. Nevertheless, the cathedral was too small for the Sienese and they started to plan the extension, wanting to turn the current cathedral into a transept. But building defects and a lack of money ruined these plans and all that remains of the scheme is a wall with a panoramic terrace on the right hand side of the cathedral.

The basilica, with its three naves, has a fairytale interior, especially the marble pulpit of Nicola Pisano with its expressive relief scenes and detailed frescoes in the *Libreria Piccolomini*. Also remarkable is the floor, decorated with marble inlays, which can unfortunately only be viewed from mid August to the end of October (additional charge 3 euros). Left from the cathedral you go down to the *Battistero San Giovanni (daily 9.30am–8pm, winter 10am–5pm)*, the baptistery whose mighty

vaults, houses some of the most important art treasures in Tuscany. During the 14th century in the Sala della Pace, Ambrogio Lorenzetti painted a series of allegories of 'good' and 'bad' governments on the first

Black and white, the colours of Siena, also decorate the Santa Maria Cathedral

pillars also contain the cathedral choir. The 15th century baptismal font was created by Jacopo della Quarcia. The main attraction in the cathedral museum *(daily 9.30am–8pm, winter 10am–5pm)* is the Maestà by Duccio Buoninsegna (1311). *Mon–Sat 10.30am–8pm, Sun 1.30pm–6pm, winter Mon–Sat 10.30am–6.30pm, Sun 1.30pm–5.30pm | 10 euros (cathedral, baptistery, panorama point and museum) | www.operaduomo.siena.it*

PALAZZO PUBBLICO

The city's town hall and its crenellated 90m/295ft high ☆ *Torre del Mangia* are stone expressions of Sienese identity and self-confidence. The brick building, with Romanesque arches and Gothic cross

floor walls. In the Sala del Mappamondo, the map room, you will find one of Siena's oldest frescoes, a Maestà (Madonna with child, 1315) and the first large format landscape representation in European painting history, named after the commander Guidoriccio (also represented in the painting) both by Simone Martini. *Daily 10am–7pm, winter until 6pm | 8 euros | Piazza del Campo 1*

PIAZZA DEL CAMPO ★

The shell-shaped piazza is famous for its beauty and architectural harmony and the unique red and white patterned brick paving that slopes down towards the town hall. As early as 1300 an urban development scheme prescribed that all the

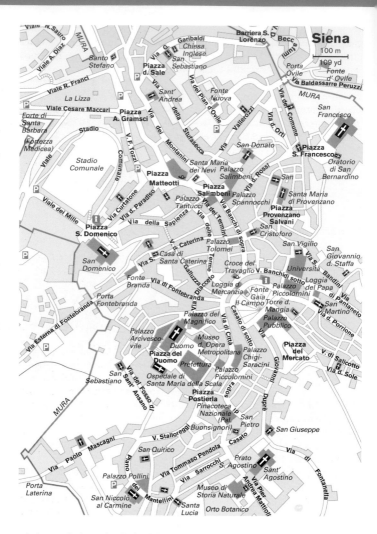

windows of the Palazzi should have the same Gothic shape as the Palazzo Pubblico. This is clearly visible in the *Palazzo Sansedoni* with its small tower. Today various restaurants and cafés with outdoor terraces surround the piazza and they are the ideal place from which to admire the view, especially of the *Fonte Gaia* which is always covered in pigeons. This rectangular fountain was created by Jacopo della Quercia in the 15th century and, after being damaged numerous times, it was redesigned in the 19th century. It is a favourite meeting spot for locals and tourists, especially when the square is in the shade.

PINACOTECA NAZIONALE DI SIENA

The patrician Buonsignori family bequeathed their beautiful city palace, with its elegant Renaissance courtyard fountain, to the province for use as a museum. It houses Siena's most important collection of paintings including works by Duccio di Buoninsegna and Simone Martini. *Tue–Sat 8.15am–7.15pm, Sun 8.15am–1.15pm, Mon 8.30am–1.30pm | 4 euros | Via San Pietro 29*

FOOD & DRINK

IL CANTO

The culinary artist, Paolo Lopriore, serves the most creative cuisine in the city in the elegant hotel Certosa di Maggiano. *Closed Tue and Wed afternoons | Strada di Certosa | tel. 05 77 28 81 82 | Expensive*

ENOTECA COMPAGNIA DEI VINATTIERI

Although wine is the main attraction here, the food is also rather fine. *Closed Mon | Via delle Terme 79 | tel. 05 77 23 65 68 | www.vinattieri.net | Moderate*

OSTERIA E ENOTECA SOTTO LE FONTI

Here you can enjoy traditional Sienese dishes like handmade pici noodles or ribollita soup. Directly opposite the Santa Caterina car park. *Closed Sun | Via Esterna Fontebranda 114 | tel. 05 77 22 64 46 | www.sottolefonti.it | Moderate*

SHOPPING

ANTICA DROGHERIA MANGANELLI

Connoisseurs and gourmets will enjoy their regional specialities. *Via di Città 71/73*

ENOTECA ITALIANA

An extensive range of top Italian wines are presented and sold in the vaults of this Medici fortress. *Mon–Sat noon–1am | Piazza Libertà 1 | www.enoteca-italiana.it*

TESSUTI FIORETTA BACCI

Scarves and jackets from the finest material, mostly handwoven. *Via San Pietro 7*

The Torre del Mangia keeps watch over the Palazzo Pubblico and the Piazza del Campo

SPORTS & ACTIVITIES

TREKKING URBANO

Favourite past time of the Sienese who like to discover the secrets of their city, like its underground water culverts, or *bottini*. Map and information available at *www.trekkingurbano.info*.

ENTERTAINMENT

In the evening it is all about seeing and being seen around the *Croce del Travaglio*, where the boulevards *Via Bianchi di Sopra*, *Via Bianchi di Sotto* and *Via di Città* converge.

AL CAMBIO
Bar and dance club, sometimes with live music, mainly for the younger crowd. *Via di Pantaneto 48 | www.alcambio.net*

WHERE TO STAY

IL CHIOSTRO DEL CARMINE
At one stage a Carmelite convent, then a student dormitory: it is now a comfortable hotel on the southern edge of the old town. *18 rooms | Via della Diana 4 | tel. 05 77 22 38 85 | www.chiostrodelcarmine.com | Moderate*

HOTEL MINERVA
This simple, well-equipped hotel is an ideal location. It is easy to reach by car and the centre is only a ten minute walk away. *56 rooms | Via Garibaldi 72 | tel. 05 77 28 44 74 | www.albergominerva.it | Budget–Moderate*

Expressive: frescoes in the Monte Oliveto Maggiore Abbey cloister

PALAZZO RAVIZZA
High ceilings, cosy lounges and a ⋇ garden with a view of the landscape make this hotel a good choice. *34 rooms | Pian dei Mantellini 34 | tel. 05 77 28 04 62 | www. palazzoravizza.it | Moderate–Expensive*

INFORMATION

Piazza del Campo 56 | tel. 05 77 28 05 51 | www.terresiena.it

WHERE TO GO

ABBAZIA DI MONTE OLIVETO MAGGIORE (148 C2) (*Ø L12*)
Located 35km/21.5mi to the south is this fortress-like abbey complex on a wind-swept hill. An imposing drawbridge gate separates the abbey, built in 1313 by the Olivetan order, from the surrounding cypress forest and outside world. The church has some beautifully engraved choir stalls with wood inlay and the massive cloister has 15th century frescoes of St Benedict painted by Luca Signorelli and Sodoma. In the *liquoreria* the friars sell herbal liqueurs. The monastery owns the simple *agritur-ismo Podere Le Piazze (6 rooms | Via delle Piazze 14 | tel. 05 77 70 72 69 | Budget)* in nearby *Chiusure di Asciano. Daily 9.15am–noon and 3.15pm–5pm, in the summer until 6pm | www.monteolivetomaggiore.it*

ABBAZIA DI SAN GALGANO (147 F2) (*Ø J13*)
Even the Russian director Andrei Tarkowski succumbed to the beauty of the vast ruins of this Cistercian abbey, 35km/21.5mi south-west of Siena, and used its massive arched nave as the set for his film 'Nostalghia'. Building of the monastery started in 1224 and its decline began around 1500. The *Trattoria Il Minestraio (closed Tue | Via del Fosso 1b | tel. 05 77 75 11 43 | Moderate)* in the neighbouring

town *Chiusdino* will win you over with their tasty dishes.

CHIANTI ★
(143 D–E 2–5) (*𝄢 K–L 8–11*)

The heart of Tuscany is wine country. On the hilly countryside between Siena and Florence the wine estates often have pictures of the black rooster – the gallo nero – the mark of quality and the emblem of the association for the local wine producers. The most fascinating aspect of this area though, is the scenery itself where pastel tones shape the landscape and cypress-lined avenues meander through vineyards, olive groves and oak forests up to fortified villages, mighty castles and magnificent villas. In the past this land belonged to patrician families who used the sharecropping system of tenant farmers. This only changed in the 20th century when the rural exodus put an end to it. Today the farmhouses often belong to foreigners or the estate owners have turned them into holiday homes for wine and cultural loving tourists. Any excursion to Chianti should include a visit to one of the wine estates along the way, such as the *Castello Fonterutoli (tel. 05 77 74 04 76 | www.fonterutoli.com)* north of Siena along the Strada Chiantigiana (SS 222) but remember to a call ahead to notify them of your visit.

About 5km/3mi further you will encounter the very touristy *Castellina in Chianti*. On the road towards San Donato in Poggio is the *Trattoria Il Fondaccio dai Dottori (daily | Via Fiorentina 73 | tel. 05 77 74 29 11 | www.ilfondaccio.com | Moderate)* serving local dishes at reasonable prices, it also has a beautiful garden. If you would like to stay longer, you can choose one of the many carefully restored farmhouses for your stay, like *Il Colombaio (13 rooms | Via Chiantigiana 29 | tel. 05 77 74 04 44 | www.albergo ilcolombaio.it | Budget)* in the north.

In Castellina, roads go off in all directions each one with a landscape prettier than the next. If you stay on the Strada Chiantigiana, drive on for 3km/1.8mi and turn off just before Greve at the junction to Lamole. Along the road is the wine estate, *Vignamaggio (Via Petriolo 5 | tel. 055 85 46 61 | www.vignamaggio.it | Expensive)*, which also rents out 23 rooms and apartments. This Renaissance villa (with garden labyrinth) is supposedly where Leonardo's Mona Lisa once lived.

Greve in Chianti (pop. 11, 000) is the Chianti region's main town. Its asymmetrically arranged *Piazza Metteotti* is lined with arches and really deserves a visit. At the narrow end of the square you can sample wine in the *Enoteca del Gallo Nero*, at no. 11 you can get tourism information, at the famous *Antica Macelleria Falorni* you can try their special salami and at no. 83 the *Ristorante Il Portico (closed Wed | tel. 05 58 54 74 26 | www.ristoranteilportico-chianti. com | Moderate)* serves the best Tuscan home cooking.

On the town's northern outskirts an exit road turns left to the *Badia a Passignano*. Monks still live behind the high abbey walls where, in the *Osteria di Passignano (closed Sun | tel. 05 58 07 12 78 | www.osteriadipassignano.com | Moderate–Expensive)*, top chef Matia Barciulli will tempt you with worldly delights (olive oil ice cream!).

From Castellina you should make a detour to ● *Radda in Chianti* (pop. 1700) where houses, palazzi and small churches cluster together behind its high village walls. The village is ☺ 'Centro Commerciale Naturale', meaning that the sausages, wine and even the colourful *Pratesi shoes (Via Chiasso dei Portici 9)* are certified 'Made in Tuscany'. This local philosophy is also evidenced in the all-female *Osteria Al Chiasso dei Portici (closed Tue | tel. 05 77 73 87 74 | Moderate)* that serves Tuscan classics like *pappa col pomodoro* and the nearby *Fattoria Poggerino (3 apartments | tel. 05 77 73 89 58 | www.poggerino.com | Moderate)*, where you can enjoy sunsets by the swimming pool.

From Radda it is 10km/6mi to the 1000 year old abbey **INSIDER TIP** *Badia a Coltibuono (April–Oct daily 2, 3, 4 and 5pm | 5 euros)* set in a magnificent forest. Walking through the wonderful gardens and the ancient Benedictine abbey itself is stepping back through history. It is now a very successful wine estate and country inn with a top-class restaurant *(10 rooms | tel. 05 77 74 48 32 | www.coltibuono.com | Moderate–Expensive)*. The SP 408 takes you back to Siena and along the way in Pievasciate is the *Parco Sculture del Chianti (April–Oct daily 10am–sunset, Nov–March by appointment only | 7.50 euros | tel. 05 77 35 71 51 | www.chiantisculpturepark.it)*, a private sculpture park that will pull you right back into the present with its contemporary art.

CHIUSI (149 F3) *(𝄞 O14)*

People come here for the treasures that are kept in the museum's neoclassical temple, the *Museo Archeologico Nazionale (daily 9am–8pm | 4 euros | Via Porsenna 93)*. The town (pop. 9000, 80km/50mi south of Siena) once belonged to the Etruscan League of 12 Cities. The museum displays give you an overview of the life and death of this ancient nation.

MONTALCINO (148 C3) *(𝄞 L13)*

For a long time this fortified village (pop. 5000, 50km/30mi south) was impregnable and it was only in 1560 that the Medici duke, Cosimo I, succeeded in occupying the last stronghold of the glorious Italian city republics. The tall and slender *Palazzo dei Priori*, on the Piazza del Popolo, is decorated with coats of arms and is a reminder of the village's great past. But the main reason people come here is to taste the award-winning red wine that has to be stored in oak barrels for four years before it can be called Brunello di Montalcino. In the *Enoteca della Fortezza (Piazzale Fortezza | www.enotecalafortezza.it)* you can get expert advice. Popular souvenirs are leather notebooks and bags by *Maledetti Toscani (Via Voltaia nel Corso 40 | www.maledettitoscani.com)*. Good home cooking, a lovely atmosphere and good prices make the **INSIDER TIP** *Taverna del Grappolo Blu (daily | Scale di Via Moglio 1 | tel. 05 77 84 71 50 | Budget–Moderate)* popular with both locals and tourists alike.

On the way between Montalcino and Castelnuovo dell'Abate lies the 12th century **INSIDER TIP** Romanesque Benedictine abbey *Sant'Antimo (Mon–Sat 10.30am–12.30pm and 3pm–6.30pm, Sun 9.15am–10.4am and 3pm–6pm)*. The rather severe basilica has a magical interior, illuminated by the sunlight that falls through its narrow windows.

MONTEPULCIANO
(149 E3) *(𝄞 N13)*

The walled vintners' town (pop. 15,000 on a hill 65km/40mi south-east of Siena) has always been very wealthy and could afford the best architects. During the 15th century Michelozzo built the town hall in the style of the Florence's Palazzo Vecchio and during the 16th century Antonio di Sangollo designed the *Palazzo Tarugi* and the *Madonna di San Biagio* church with its distinctive cupola. Besides the red wine Vino Nobile di Montepulciano (which previously only the nobility were allowed to produce), the music and theatre festival *Cantiere Internazionale dell'Arte (www.fondazionecantiere.it)* at the end of July/beginning of August, now also attracts a lot of visitors to the town. The *Caffè Poliziano (daily | Via Voltaia del Corso*

27/29 | www.caffepoliziano.it) is easily one of the most beautiful cafés in Tuscany, and the *Enoteca la Bottega del Nobile (Via di Gracciano nel Corso 93 | www.vinonobile. eu)* the most beautiful wine cellar in the town.

principles in urban design that reflected clarity and rationality. Ideas that came into play when Pope Pius II commissioned the Renaissance architect Bernardo Rossellino in 1460 to transform his home town into the 'ideal city'. First of all he

A sea of roofs: the warm hues of Montepulciano match the colour of the Vino Nobile

MONTERIGGIONI (142 C5) (*J11*)

On a hill 10km/6mi north is this fortified medieval village. Its towers, erected in 1203, were described by Dante as looking like 'giants guarding the gates of hell'. The village (pop. 9000) is full of atmosphere, especially at the beginning of July during the medieval festival Di Torre Si Corona. In the only hotel within the walls, the *Hotel Monteriggioni (12 rooms | Via 1° Maggio 4 | tel. 05 77 30 50 09 | www.hotel monteriggioni.net | Expensive),* transports one to another world.

PIENZA (149 D3) (*M13*)

After the mystical Middle Ages, man was once again allowed to be the focus and this meant that there were some new

designed an outdoor community square, the Piazza Pio II. Around it he arranged the bishop's palace (Palazzo Piccolomini), the city hall with its arches, and the spacious cathedral. He used an optical trick – the sides of the square make a trapezoid – giving the illusion of volume.

An osteria that is a culinary must is the *Sette di Vino (closed Mon | Piazza di Spagna 1 | tel. 05 78 74 90 92 | Moderate)* serving delicious local specialities. In Camprena 6km/3.7mi further north, is a rather special place to stay, **INSIDER TIP** *Agriturismo Sant'Anna (43 rooms | district Sant'Anna in Camprena | tel. 05 79 74 80 37 | www. camprena.it | Moderate),* a former monastery that was the location for the film 'The English Patient'.

SAN GIMIGNANO ★
(142 B4) (*ⓂH10*)

The higher, the more powerful: this town (pop. 7000, 45km/28mi north-west) owes its landmarks to this medieval contest of vanity. The almost 54m/177ft high towers, of which 15 have been preserved, are the reason that millions of tourist come to this fortified town. As soon as the fuss is over at night, the medieval streets and cobbled squares belong to the locals again.

On the main square, the *Piazza della Cisterna* with its travertine fountain, is the eponymous hotel and restaurant *(50 rooms | tel. 05 77 94 03 28 | www.hotel cisterna.it | Moderate)* that has had a good reputation for many years and in the *Gelateria di Piazza (daily)* a master ice cream maker is at work. The Piazza Duomo, is full of medieval gems, that you should not miss: the *Santa Maria Assunta* (1148) church with its frescoes and its broad staircase, the *Loggia del Battistero* with the mural from the workshop of Domenico Ghilandaio (1476), the 12th century *Palazzo Vecchio del Podestà* with its large archway and the coat of arms bedecked *Palazzo del Popolo,* where the city museum is housed. It has the same opening times *(summer daily 9.30am–7pm, winter 10am–5.30pm | 5 euros)* as the ⚡ *Torre Grossa* next door which has a panoramic view over the whole Elsa Valley. The 13th century monastery *Sant'Agostino,* with its famous frescoes by Benozzo Gozzoli, can be reached via the Via San Matteo and the Via Cellolese.

Amongst the town's craftsmen, Franco Balducci stands out with his exquisite ceramic designs: INSIDER TIP *Ceramiche Aristica Balducci (Piazza delle Erbe 5 | www. francobalducci.com)*. In the *Osteria del Carcere (closed Wed | Via del Castello 10 | tel. 05 77 94 19 05 | Moderate)* you are served – typically Tuscan – soup as *primo* instead of pasta.

VAL D'ORCIA ★
(148–149 C–D 3) (*ⓂM13–14*)

The unique landscape south of Siena is known as *le Crete Senesi* because of its characteristic clay soil which dries out during the summer. The sandy and barren landscape holds a magnetic fascination. In places the lunar landscape – which is interwoven with wheat fields, vineyards and olive groves – has hardly changed in centuries. Instead of new buildings, traffic and industrial sites, here one sees endless rolling hills, tall cypresses, isolated farmsteads, ancient monasteries and medieval mountain strongholds. Today the expansive valley between Buonconvento, Monte Amiata and Montepulciano is Parco Artistico, Naturale e Culturale della Val d'Orcia *(www.parcodellavaldorcia.com)* a nature and cultural park and Unesco world heritage site. The landscape is, as stated in the explanatory statement, a result of the constant and well thought-out actions of man.

The park headquarters are in the beautiful village of *San Quirico d'Orcia*. During the summer they organise a festival with music, dance, theatre and film. Along the border of the town are some ancient thermal baths ideal for you to revive your body and mind, which is also something you can do at the *Hotel Posta Marcucci (36 rooms | tel. 05 77 88 71 12 | www.hotel postamarcucci.it | Moderate–Expensive)* in *Bagno Vignoni*. The open thermal baths from the Middle Ages may no longer be in use but the modern versions will certainly do the trick.

VOLTERRA ★
(141 F5) (*ⓂG11*)

This town (pop. 12,000) perched in a harsh, volcanic landscape, thrives on tourism and alabaster. During Etruscan times it was known as Velathri and belonged to the powerful League of 12 Cities. After that the name cropped up once again about half a millennia later when, as a free commune, it had to submit to Florence in 1530. Today the wind and weather are this town's enemy: they erode the *balze*, the clay and volcanic layers on which the town was built.

oldest town hall in Tuscany, the *Palazzo Priori* (1208–54,) and the *Palazzo Pretorio*, also from the 13th century with a tower and loggia. To get to the 4th century *Arco Etrusco*, one of the few surviving Etruscan city gates, you need to cross the Piazza San Giovanni. It is worth stopping on the

From kitsch to art: alabaster souvenirs are ubiquitous in Volterra

The town is a good 50km/31mi from Siena and you enter the fortified old town through the Porta Selci at the Medici fortress. Just behind it is the *Museo Etrusco Guarnacci (daily 9am–7pm, in the winter 9am–1.30pm | 8 euros | Via Don Minzoni 15)*. The collection includes the thin bronze statuette, *Ombra della Sera* (Evening Shadow) and also the symbol of Etruscan art, the sarcophagus depicting a married couple. Nearby, in house no.70, local cuisine is served in the friendly atmosphere of the *Trattoria Ombra della Sera (closed Mon | tel. 05 88 88 66 63 | Moderate)*
From the Via Gramsci turn right to the *Roman Theatre*, which is still being used as a summer stage, and left along the Via Matteotti to the beautifully preserved *Piazza dei Priori*. Here you can see the

piazza to take in the 12th century *Santa Maria Assunta* Cathedral and its octagonal baptistery.
Volterra is also famous for its alabaster workshops that line the road. The **INSIDER TIP** family owned business *Rossi* at *Via del Mandorlo 7 (www.rossialabastri. com)* has the best reputation. The popular Twilight saga has a fictional royal vampire family that lived in Volterra which has now also become a Mecca for fans of the series who flock here for the **INSIDER TIP** *New Moon Tour (30 euros | www.newmoon officialtour.com)*. The best place to recuperate after your vampire tour is in the large park belonging to the hotel *Villa Nencini (34 rooms | Borgo Santo Stefano 55 | tel. 058 88 63 86 | www.villanencini.it | Budget–Moderate)*.

MAREMMA & COSTA DEGLI ETRUSCHI

This area is a region of incomparable natural beauty, full of ancient traditions and brimming with Tuscan culture. It has a wonderfully varied coastline – at times rocky and rugged, then gentle and sandy or lined with pine trees – with magnificent beaches and picturesque harbours. The hinterland is just as varied – lush vegetation alternating between hills and cultivated plains, then mountainous and wild – with small villages huddled around medieval castles. The provinces of Grosseto and Livorno along the Tyrrhenian Sea offer a fascinating blend of diverse nature, magnificent culture and a wide choice of outdoor activities.

GROSSETO

(150 B1) *(*ⓜ *J16)* **Tourism arrived relatively late to the province but it was settled way back by the Etruscans who found it to be a land rich in mineral resources.**
One problem was that the area was marshland, made all the more inhospitable by malaria. This only changed in the 20th century when the area was successfully drained resulting in large tracts of fertile land. The province quickly became the vegetable garden for the region. This is also the reason why there are so many vendors selling their *frutta e verdura* along

Photo: Porto Ercole yacht marina in Monte Argentario

Medieval villages, museums, mines and the magnificent Etruscan coast: this is Tuscany's holiday paradise

the roads. During the Middle Ages the provincial capital (pop. 80,000, 10km/ 6mi from the coast) was the bishop's seat. Up until 2001 vehicles blocked the view from the historic buildings of the old town but today locals and tourists are able to stroll through the renovated town centre, with its broad arcades, and drink espresso at outdoor cafés or stroll along the chic Corso Carducci.

FORTEZZA MEDICEA

You can walk around the broad walls of the hexagonal ramparts that date back to the 16th century. During its construction, the old citadel *(Cassero Senese | summer Tue–Sat 10am–8pm, Sun 10am–1pm and 5pm–8pm, winter Tue–Sun 10am–6pm)* was integrated into the new town walls. The moat around the city wall was in use until 1835 when it was filled in and turned into parks and streets.

MUSEO ARCHEOLOGICO E D'ARTE DELLA MAREMMA

The local museum for archaeology and art is full of treasures that capture the splendour and the customs of Maremma's Etruscans. *Summer Tue–Sat 10am–8pm, Sun 10am–1pm and 5pm–8pm, winter Tue–Sun 10am–6pm | 5 euros | Piazza Baccarini 3 | www.archeologiatoscana.it*

standing contribution to the reclamation of Maremma.

FOOD & DRINK

LA BUCA DI SAN LORENZO

This restaurant, in the city wall, has for years been regarded as one of the best in the city. Host Claudio Musu never rests on his laurels and always comes up with new combinations. *Closed Sun/Mon | Viale Manetti 1 | tel. 0 56 42 51 42 | Moderate–Expensive*

Lots of space on the wide sandy stretch of the Marina di Grosseto beach

PIAZZA DANTE

In the 19th century the city gave its central square an historic renovation. The 14th century Romanesque-Gothic cathedral received a marble façade in the medieval Sienese style, the new town hall was built in the style of the Gothic Florentine palaces and the new provincial administration building was modelled on Siena's town hall. The monument in the centre of the square is dedicated to the Duke of Lorraine, Leopold II, who made an out-

FIUMARA BEACH

A young team serve seafood dishes right on the beach during summer. Book in advance – and do not forget your bug spray! In the Marina di Grosseto district. *Daily | district Fiumara | tel. 0 56 43 40 40 | www.fiumarabeach.it | Moderate*

ROSSO E VINO

A mix between a restaurant and an *enoteca* where guests are spoiled with creative regional dishes and some of the best wines of the region. *Closed Tue | Piazza Pacciardi 2 | tel. 05 64 41 12 09 | Moderate*

SHOPPING

INSIDERTIP CANTINA VINI DI MAREMMA ●
If you want to take a bit of Maremma home with you, you should pay a visit to the cooperative on the SS 332. The culinary specialities come from the farmers in the region. *Il Cristo district | Marina di Grosseto | www.ivinidimaremma.it*

MERCATO SETTIMANALE
Every Thursday morning the weekly market along the city wall is lined with stalls selling clothing and home wares. *Piazza del Mercato*

ACTIVITIES & BEACHES

HORSE COUNTRY MAREMMA
This is a land of horseback adventure and cowboys, the *butteri,* and it has everything to delight horse lovers: trail rides, gallops along the beach, carriage rides and more. *Equinus | Via dell'Unione 37 | tel. 0 56 42 49 88 | www.cavallomaremmano.it*

BEACH LIFE
Sunbathing, kitesurfing, paddling, and sailing: during the summer the coastal village of Marina di Grosseto becomes one large outdoor recreational park where you can choose between a public beach and a manicured lido *(bagno).* The dogs' beach is just behind the *Fiumara Bridge.* Information: *www.marinadigrosseto.it*

ENTERTAINMENT

PUB IRISH SOUL
The pub, in the city's oldest house, stocks a wide range of good European beers so even in the middle of the Tuscan wine lands there are people who appreciate a beer! *Daily | Piazza del Mercato 23 | www.irishsoulpub.it*

WHERE TO STAY

FATTORIA DEL BACCINELLO
Although this chic estate, with restaurant and swimming pool, is 25km/15.5mi east

⭐ **Massa Marittima**
A medieval town that is a work of art → p. 76

⭐ **Il Giardino di Daniel Spoerri**
The highly personal sculpture park is another form of autograph album
→ p. 74

⭐ **Parco Regionale della Maremma**
Home to some traditional Tuscan 'cowboys' → p. 75

⭐ **Pitigliano**
Perched on a yellow stone ridge is Tuscany's 'Little Jerusalem' → p. 78

⭐ **Sovana**
The most impressive Etruscan ruins in Tuscany
→ p. 79

⭐ **Bolgheri**
Images of the cypress-lined avenue are often used to promote Tuscany → p. 82

⭐ **Parco Archeologico di Baratti e Populonia**
A Tuscan Pompei → p. 83

MARCO POLO HIGHLIGHTS

in Baccinelo, the trip is well worth it. *6 rooms, 6 apartments | tel. 0 56 41 91 15 69 | www.fattoriadelbaccinello.com | Moderate*

LOLA PICCOLO HOTEL

With the renovation of their beach hotel, the Ferroni family opted for functional design and pastel colours. The hotel has a private beach. *36 rooms | Via XXIV Maggio 39 | Marina di Grosseto | tel. 0 56 43 44 02 | www.lolahotel.it | Moderate–Expensive*

INFORMATION

During summer: *Corso Carducci 1 | tel. 05 64 48 82 08;* otherwise: *Via Monte Rosa 206 | tel. 0 56 44 62 61 | www.turismo inmaremma.it*

WHERE TO GO

CASTIGLIONE DELLA PESCAIA
(147 D6) (*M G16*)

Typical Mediterranean holiday atmosphere and an award-winning beach with crystal clear water are just two of the advantages of this harbour village (pop. 7500) 22km/14mi west. A thick line of pine trees shelters the mile-long sandy beach, white yachts gently bob alongside the pier and colourful fishing boats bring in their fresh catch daily. The fresh fish is excellently prepared at *Romolo (closed Tue | Corso della Libertà 10 | tel. 05 64 93 35 33 | Moderate–Expensive).* Along the beach promenade one bagno is squeezed in next to the other and in the evening holidaymakers stroll along the promenade past bars, shops, restaurants and the popular **INSIDER TIP** *Gelateria Paradise (daily 10am–2am | Via Vittorio Veneto 13)* that serves the creamiest ice cream in the area. The *Hotel Miramare (37 rooms | Via Vittorio Veneto 35 | tel. 05 64 93 35 24 | www.hotelmiramare.info | Moderate)* is situated right on the sea, and everything

is watched over by the fortified village above, where you will feel as though you have stepped back in time to the Middle Ages.

IL GIARDINO DEI TAROCCHI
(151 E4) (*M L18*)

A fantasy sculpture garden with 22 colourful Tarot symbols that seem to grow out of the ground. The French artist Niki de Saint Phalle (1930–2002) was commissioned to create the garden. To visit the garden you have to travel 60km/37mi to the south and leave the four-lane coastal road Aurelia at the Pescia Fiorentina exit. *April–mid Oct daily 2.30pm–7.30pm, Nov–March 1st Sat of the month 9am–1pm | 10.50 euros, free Nov–March | www.nikidesaintphalle. com*

IL GIARDINO DI DANIEL SPOERRI ★
(148 C4) (*M L14*)

In his sculpture garden, on the northern slopes of Monte Amiata in Seggiano 65km/40mi north-east of Grosseto, the Swiss sculptor Daniel Spoerri displays his own sculptures and those of his friends. Here one of Jean Tinguely's scrap machines

rumbles into life at the press of a button, Jesús Soto's sound sculpture whistles in the wind and visitors trip over bronze slippers cast by Spoerri himself. *Easter–June and mid Sept–Oct Tue–Sun, July–mid Sept daily 11am–8pm, Nov–Easter by appointment only | 10 euros | tel. 05 64 95 08 05 | www.danielspoerri.org*

MAREMMA
(150 A–B 1–3) (*⌕ H–J 16–17*)

Scenic landscapes, crystal clear water, miles of fine sandy beaches, shady pine groves, villages steeped in history and a sun smiling from the azure blue sky almost all year round: just some of the many reasons why this stretch of coast between Grosseto and the Monte Argentario peninsula has become a holiday paradise. Add to this the many holiday farmhouses such as the *Fattoria La Capitana (5 apartments | Via Sterpeti 1 | tel. 05 64 50 77 70 | www.laca pitana.it | Moderate)* in Maglione or the wine estate and spa, *Antico Casale (24 rooms | district Castagneta | tel. 05 64 50 72 19 | www.anticocasalediscansano.it | Expensive)* in Scansano which promises authenticity and quality.

At the heart of this region is the ★☺ *Parco Regionale della Maremma*, a nature reserve between the Ombrone estuary and the Talamone harbour. The park is home to wild game and some cattle from the farm *Azienda di Alberese (www.alberese. com)* that are watched over by herdsmen on horseback. Visitors have to enter the park at the entrances at Talamone and Alberese and must stay on the roads. Information about tours, night walks and ● **INSIDER TIP** canoe trips can be obtained in the visitor centre in Alberese *(Centro Visite Alberese | June–Sept daily 8am–8.30pm, Oct–May 8.30am–1.30pm | Via Bersagliere 7/9 | tel. 05 64 40 70 98 | www. naturalmentetoscana.it)*. On the website you will also find a list with accommodation in the park grounds. Just like the park, the restaurant *Da Remo (closed Wed | Rispescia Stazione 5/7 | tel. 05 64 40 50 14 | Moderate)* has hardly changed over the years, especially with regard to the quality of its fish dishes.

The Maremma may be attractive because of its scenery and pristine nature but it is also ideal for outdoor enthusiasts and culture lovers alike who will feel at home

Talamone forms the southern border of the Maremma nature reserve

here – golf, biking, walking, jazz concerts and folklore events – where there is something for everyone. Information: *Viale Monte Rosa 206 | Grosseto | tel. 05 64 46 26 11 | www.turismoinmaremma.it*

MASSA MARITTIMA ★
(147 D3) (*Ω G13–14*)

It is easy to lose your heart to this medieval mining town (pop. 9000 50km/31mi to the north): an aperitif at sunset on the Piazza Garibaldi, the view over the vast countryside to the sea from the ☙ defence tower *Torre del Candeliere (summer Tue–Sun 10am–1pm and 3pm–6pm, winter 11am–1pm and 2.30pm–4.30pm | 2.50 euros)* on the Piazza Matteotti and a stroll through the alleyways of the Romanesque lower town up to the Gothic upper town Città Nuova. The fact that the town centre is so well preserved is because malaria forced its citizens to flee during the 15th century. The town lay, like a Sleeping

Beauty, for four centuries before people began to return to it. The *Piazza Garibaldi* in the lower Città Vecchia is the centre and can be reached from the Piazzale Mazzini in the east. There, surrounded by travertine palaces and perched on a platform, is the beautiful cathedral, *San Cerbone* with its wonderful 11th century Christian reliefs.

A few steps further in the *Taverna del Vecchio Borgo (closed Sun evening and Mon | Via Parenti 12 | tel. 05 66 90 39 50 | Moderate–Expensive)* they serve typical game dishes. 10km/6mi south of the city is *Tenuta del Fontino (25 rooms, 6 apartments | district Accesa | tel. 05 66 91 92 32 | www.tenutafontino.it | Moderate)*, a wine estate with swimming pool, lake and horseback riding.

MONTE AMIATA ☺
(149 D5) (*Ω M15*)

On clear days, the characteristic cone shape of the extinct volcano (1738m/5702ft) can be seen throughout Tuscany. Nevertheless, its remote, lushly forested slopes are a well-kept secret. For centuries, the population here has lived on its

The Piazza Garibaldi in Massa Marittima's Città Vecchia is seldom this empty

mineral resources but since the cinnabar mine closed during the 1970s, the area has started to rely on sustainable, eco-tourism with plant and animal protection areas being set up, as well as a dense network of themed hiking trails, amongst them the INSIDER TIP chestnut trail, *Strada del Castagno*. The journey into the spectacular landscape is an encounter with a culture many centuries old.

Free hiking maps are available in the *tourist office (Via Adua 25 | tel. 05 77 77 58 11 | www.amiataturismo.it)* in the main village *Abbadia San Salvatore* (pop. 7000, 75km/46.5mi east of Grosseto) on the eastern flanks of the Monte Amiata. There it is worth visiting the oldest Tuscan *abbey (daily 7am–8pm)* dating back to the year 750, with a crypt supported by 36 columns and the *mine museum (Museo Minerario | mid June–Oct daily 9.30am–12.30pm and 3.30pm–6.30pm, or by appointment | 6 euros | Piazzale Rossaro 6 | tel. 05 77 77 83 24 | www.museominerario.it),* where the history of cinnabar mining is documented. The hotel and restaurant *Fabbrini (35 rooms | Via Cavour 53 | tel. 05 77 77 99 11 | www.hotelfabbrini.com | Budget–*

Moderate) in an old city villa, has simple, yet comfortable accommodation.

The most beautiful place (pop. 3000) on Monte Amiata is *Santa Fiora*, enter the village from the south and just after the bridge, on the Piazza Garibaldi, you will come across the oldest part of the village the *Castello* with the remains of a castle, a clock tower and a Sforza family Renaissance palace. The Via Carolina leads you to *Al Barilotto (closed Wed | Via Carolina 24 | tel. 05 64 97 70 89 | Moderate)* where you can order tasty local food, in the *borgo* at the foot of the Castello. *Montecatino* lies just outside the city walls and is famous for the giant fish pond from the 15th century, the *Peschiera*, which collects water from the Fiora River.

MONTE ARGENTARIO
(150 B–C 4–5) (*ω J18–19*)

Turquoise water, white sandy bays and rugged cliffs line the promontory 45km/28mi to the south. A saltwater lagoon has formed between two spits of land *(tomboli)* that connect the island to the mainland. Here flamingos winter in a ☺ WWF oasis (only Sept–April Sat/Sun 9.30am–

3.30pm | 5 euros | entrance Via Aurelia at km 148.3). The family-friendly *Villa La Parrina (12 rooms, 3 apartments | district La Parrina | tel. 05 64 86 26 36 | www. parrina.it | Moderate–Expensive)* is situated nearby.

The Ildebranda tomb in Sovana: carved into tuff stone 4000 years ago

The old harbour village of *Orbetello* – on a headland, which juts from the mainland into the lagoon – is connected to the foothills by an artificial dam. It has a noteworthy cathedral and a rustic fish restaurant, *I Pescatori (summer daily, winter Mon–Fri closed | Via Leopardi 9 | tel. 05 64 86 06 11 | Moderate)* run by local fishermen, where you can also buy the smoked fish eggs speciality **INSIDERTIP** *bottarga*.

On the right hand side of the peninsula is *Porto Santo Stefano,* where the ⚐ coast-

al road, *Strada Panoramica,* starts that will take you to the harbour, *Porto Ercole,* on the other side. The surrounding dense forest hides some villas belonging to VIPs and the Porto Ercole the luxury hotel *Il Pellicano (50 rooms, 15 suits | district Sbarcatello | tel. 05 64 85 81 11 | www. pellicanohotel.com | Expensive).*

PITIGLIANO ★
(151 F2) *(⌂ M17)*
When this village emerges suddenly (70km/43.5mi to the south-east) it takes your breath away. It seems to grow right out the 300m/980ft high tuff rock ridge that is stands on. Its 3500 year old history has been written by the Etruscans, the Romans and – during the Middle Ages – by the aristocratic Orsini family. The town centre, behind the massive aqueduct, is a labyrinth of alleys and stairs, where in the Middle Ages Spanish Jews found refuge. Reminders of this are **INSIDERTIP** the *cemetery,* a *synagogue* and a *museum (Sun–Fri 10am–1.30pm and 2.30pm–6.30pm, winter 10am–12.30pm and 3pm–5.30pm | 3 euros | Vicolo Marghera)* as well as a *pastry shop (Via Zuccarelli 167)* with kosher delicacies. The restaurant *Il Grillo (closed Tue | Via Cavour 18 | tel. 05 64 61 52 02 | Budget)* specialises in hearty traditional dishes.

INSIDERTIP SATURNIA **(151 E2)** *(⌂ L17)*
People come here for the hot sulphur springs that bubble out of the volcanic crater, 60km/37mi east of Grosseto. The luxury hotel built around the Roman spa *(Terme di Saturnia | 140 rooms | district Follonata | tel. 05 64 60 01 110 | www. termedisaturnia.it | Expensive)* also welcomes day visitors. The flowing water cascades into a ● waterfall, *Cascata del Mulino,* flowing in stages into a natural stone basin where you can enjoy its benefits free of charge.

SORANO
(151 F1–2) (*M16*)

Carved into rock this medieval village (pop. 3700, 80km/50mi east of Grosseto) is one of the most impressive that the south-east of Tuscany has to offer. It is terraced around a massive rock, and each of its narrow, winding streets, with residential towers and picturesque courtyards, are worth exploring. In the thick walls of the *castle* (built in 1550) that towers over the village, is the atmospheric *Hotel della Fortezza | 16 rooms | Piazza Cairoli | tel. 05 64 63 20 10 | www.fortezzahotel.it | Moderate*

SOVANA ★
(151 F2) (*M17*)

Wars and catastrophes left the village in a state of neglect, but the careful modernization and preservation of buildings have brought it back to life again. The hotel and restaurant *La Taverna Etrusca (closed Wed | 18 rooms | Piazza Pretorio | tel. 05 64 61 41 13 | www.sovana.eu | Moderate–Expensive)* on the cobbled village square is steeped in historic charm. In the 11th century the Aldobrandeschi family expanded the original Etruscan settlement into a gigantic fortress, and it was also here a future pope was born. Do not miss out on the village's Romanesque cathedral as well as the ● *Parco Archeologico Città del Tufo (mid March–Oct daily 10am–7pm, Nov–mid March Fri–Sun 9am–5pm | 5 euros | www.leviecave.it)* on the SP 22 in the direction of San Martino. There you will find the 3rd century tomb, *Tomba Ildebranda* with its columns and stairs hewn into the rock, as well as *Il Cavone*, a deep road carved into the soft tuff stone. Don't forget your comfortable shoes! Take home some Etruscan culture in the form of jewellery reproductions from *Arte Etrusca | closed Wed | Via del Duomo 24.*

VETULONIA (147 D–E5) (*H15*)

We have Isidoro Falchi, a doctor with a penchant for archaeology, to thank for the discovery of the Etruscan town of Vatl. He stumbled upon the tombs, in the medieval hamlet 22km/14mi to the northwest, in 1892. Since then, the ground has revealed many settlement remains. In the *Museo Civico Archeologico (June–Sept Tue–Sun 10am–2pm and 4pm–8pm, Oct–Feb 10am–4pm, March–May 10am–6pm | 4.50 euros)* at the entrance to the village you can see the burial objects. Not with Etruscan, but with medieval recipes, Francesco Angeloni in the **INSIDER TIP** *Osteria Il Cantuccio (closed Mon | Piazza Indipendenza 31 | tel. 05 64 94 80 11 | Moderate)* in the neighbouring village of *Buriano* has cooked his way into the hearts of his regular guests.

LIVORNO

(140 B3–4) (*D9*) Many only know this harbour city (population 161,000) as the gateway to Elba, Corsica and Sardinia but Tuscany's second largest city it does not deserve this! Although

---

CITY **WHERE TO START?**
Start with a stroll along the seaside promenade **Viale Italia**. You can leave your vehicle at the parking area on the Piazza Mazzini in front of the Nuova Darsena docks and take the bus number 1 to the Mascagni observation platform and to the aquarium. In the opposite direction, the bus line number 1 goes to the central Piazza Grande, from where you can comfortably reach the Quartiere Venezia and the two Medici fortresses.

it does not have an old town full of Renaissance palaces and medieval alleys, it does have lovely broad streets where the sunlight reaches into the furthest corners and good-humoured and happy citizens.

Livorno gained importance during the 16th century when Florentine's powerful Medici family needed access to the sea. In order to lure wealthy Jews there, they also passed laws to allow freedom of speech and religious tolerance. This is the reason behind the city's ethnic mix.

SIGHTSEEING

INSIDER TIP ACQUARIO COMUNALE ●

The city aquarium, in front of the cobbled Terrazza Mascagni, has about 65 tanks offering some exciting insights into the underwater world of the Mediterranean. *Summer Tue–Sun 10am–6pm, winter Sat/ Sun 10am–6pm, Thu 2pm–6pm | 12 euros | Viale Italia*

FORTEZZA VECCHIA AND FORTEZZA NUOVA

The Medici's reinforced their outpost along the coast by building this pentagon-shaped brick fortress in 1521. A good 50 years later, the Grand Duke Ferdinand I ordered another stronghold to be built, the Fortezza Nuova and had the two forts connected by a ring canal, the Fosso Reale. The Fortezza Nuova *(entrance until 7.30pm via Scala Fortezza Nuova in the south)* now serves as an urban green space.

LUNGOMARE

As soon as the sun appears this 4km/2.5mi long seaside promenade – between the bathing beach Scoglia della Regina and the circular pine grove Rotonda Ardenza – fills up with pedestrians, cyclists and joggers. Along the way is the 🎭 *Mascagni terrace,* with art nouveau villas, bars and cafés. In the evening the promenade is full of people strolling or enjoying a stop at the *barac-chine* for a *gelato* or an aperitif.

Livorno's catch of the day forms the basis of the *cacciucco,* a local variant of bouillabaisse

INSIDERTIP ▶ MUSEO CIVICO GIOVANNI FATTORI

During the 19th century the local artist Giovanni Fattori was a leading member of the 'Macchiaioli' group – Tuscany's answer to the French Impressionists – artworks by Fattori and others of the style are on display in the art nouveau Villa Mimbelli. *Tue–Sun 10am–1pm and 4pm–7pm | 4 euros | Via San Jacopo in Acquaviva 63*

QUARTIERE VENEZIA NUOVA

The heart of the city pulsates in this old fishing and trade quarter between the two Medici forts. It is made up of a network of canals lined with restaurants and artists' studios and shops. Like Venice, it is built on wooden stilts. On the waterways the vaulted arcades from the 17th century, that extend below the houses, were used as storage areas for the city's treasures, they can be **INSIDERTIP** explored by boat *Giro in Battello | 10 euros | tickets in the Punto Informazioni | Via Pieroni 18.*

FOOD & DRINK

ANTICA TORTERIA DA GAGARIN

For the best *cecina* – a local pancake made from chickpea flour – in town try this snack bar behind the market hall. *Mon–Sat 8am–2pm and 3pm–8pm | Via Cardinale 24 | Budget*

IL SOTTOMARINO

Host Fulvio Beni serves specialities from the region in his authentic restaurant. *Closed Mon/Tue | Via Terrazzini 48 | tel. 05 86 88 70 25 | Moderate*

TRATTORIA UNDICI

Livornians are of the opinion that this *trattoria* serves the best *cacciucco*, a delicious creamy fish stew. *Closed Mon | Via Bassa 8 | tel. 05 86 88 03 04 | Moderate*

SHOPPING

GIANNI CUCCUINI

When locals need an outfit for a special occasion this is their first stop in the pedestrian zone. *Via Ricasoli 35*

MERCATINO DEL VENERDÌ

A paradise for bargain hunters. *Fri 8am–1.30pm | Via dei Pensieri*

MERCATO CENTRALE

Large, iron and stone art nouveau market hall with a choice of 180 stalls selling everything that is used in Mediterranean cuisine. *Mon–Fri 5am–2pm, Sat 5am–7pm | Via del Cardinale/Via Buontalenti*

SPORTS & ACTIVITIES

SAILING

In the *Aquaria Natura Club (Via Magenta 12 | tel. 33 85 01 05 13 | www.aquarianatura. it)* you can learn how to handle sails and spinnakers or you can book a sailing trip with a skipper.

SCUBA DIVING SCHOOL

Take a dive course with the *Accademia Blu Diving Center (Bagni Pancaldi | Viale Italia 62 | tel. 05 86 26 00 70 | www.accademia blu.net)*.

ENTERTAINMENT

BAR CIVILI

Artists paid for their *ponce*, a local beverage made with coffee and rum, with paintings which then decorate the walls of the restaurant. *Closed Sun | Via della Vigna 55*

FORTEZZA VECCHIA

Between May and September cultural events take place almost daily in the old fortress. *Entrance Stazione Marittima*

LIVORNO

WHERE TO STAY

GRAND HOTEL PALAZZO

Here the glorious belle époque era continues in the 21st century but the comforts are all very modern. *123 rooms Viale Italia 195 | tel. 05 86 26 08 36 | www.grandhotel palazzo.it | Expensive*

HOTEL AL TEATRO

This mid range hotel impresses with its central location and beautiful courtyard where you can breakfast during summer. Garage parking possible. *8 rooms | Via Enrico Mayer 42 | tel. 05 86 89 87 05 | www.hotelalteatro.it | Moderate*

INFORMATION

Piazza Municipio and *Via Pieroni 18 | tel. 05 86 20 46 11 | www.costadeglietruschi.it*

WHERE TO GO

BOLGHERI ★
(146 B1) (*ɯ F12*)

Situated 52km/32mi to the south, the drive along the famous 5km/3mi cypress-lined avenue up to the city walls is a rhapsody in green, while the medieval hamlet behind the city gate is a world in red. The village, that was the seat of the Gherardesca family, is now very popular with tourists. A good address is the *Taverna del Pittore (closed Mon | Largo Nonna Lucia 4 | tel. 05 65 76 21 84 | Moderate–Expensive)* where local dishes are served on the terrace during the summer and in their lounge, with a fireplace, during winter.

CAMPIGLIA MARITTIMA
(146 B3) (*ɯ F13*)

Most visitors choose to simply wander through the picturesque alleys of this beautiful hilltop town (pop. 13,000) 75km/

46.5mi to the south. Both the 13th century *Palazzo Pretorio* bedecked in coats of arms and the Romanesque church *Pieve San Giovanni* deserve special mention. In the medieval heart of the town the *Locanda Il Canovaccio (Via Vecchio Asilo 1 | tel. 05 65 83 84 49 | www.locandailcano vaccio.it)*, an elegant bed and breakfast *(3 rooms | Moderate)* with a excellent restaurant *(Sept–June closed Tue | Moderate–Expensive)* is a good choice.

CASTIGLIONCELLO
(140 B5) (*ɯ D11*)

This village (pop. 3500, 27km/16mi to the south) was once a fashionable bathing resort during the 19th century, when Florentine nobles built their summer villas on the cliffs with private access to the bays. During the 1970s and 1980s it was the meeting place for Rome's jet-set crowd. Today the summer fun has been democratised, albeit with very high prices. There is a very beautiful ⬚ coastal promenade that goes to the neighbouring village Rosignano and an elegant holiday resort ⬚ *Casale del Mare (7 apartments | Strada Vicinale delle Spinate | tel. 05 85 75 90 07 | www.casaledelmare.it | Expensive)* with pool, tennis court and wonderful sea views.

COSTA DEGLI ETRUSCHI
(140 B–C 4–6, 146 A1–4)
(*ɯ D–E 10–14*)

The 90km/50mi long coastal stretch between Livorno and Piombine promises the best kind of holiday fun with its sand and pebble beaches for sun lovers and rocky cliffs for snorkelers. There are some family-friendly holiday resorts, in amongst the pine forests, which offer various activities while in the hilly hinterland there are villages where the smell of the sea blends alluringly with an ancient past. *www.costadeglietruschi.it*

MUSEO DELLA GEOTERMIA DI LARDERELLO (147 D1) (*M G12*)

Some 85km/50mi south-east is the world's oldest geothermal plant with a network of metal tubes where hot steam from the earth is converted into electricity. The plant's museum documents the history of this pioneering sustainable energy plant. *Mid March–Oct daily 9.30am–6.30pm, Nov–mid March Tue–Sun 10am–5pm | free admission | Piazza Leopolda*

PARCO ARCHEOLOGICO DI BARATTI E POPULONIA ★ ● (146 A4) (*M E14*)

The medieval Populonia, 75km/46.5mi to the south, on a rocky ledge above the INSIDER TIP Gulf of Baratti, was an important Etruscan iron smelting centre. Their kilns were situated down on the coast. When researchers removed layers of slag during the 20th century, they found necropolises, tombs and workshops. Today the site is accessible as an *Archaeology Park (summer daily 9am–8pm, winter Tue–Fri 9am–2pm, Sat/Sun 9am–5pm | 15 euros, Nov–Feb 9 euros | www.parchivaldicornia.it)*. The wide sweeping bay with fine white sand and crystal clear water is one of the most beautiful beaches in Tuscany. Large umbrella pines provide shade, fishing boats bob in the small harbour, and still you only have to pay for the parking, not to swim. Exquisite fish dishes are served at the restaurant *Il Lucumone (closed Mon | Via San Giovanni di Sotto 24 | tel. 05 65 29 47 1 | Moderate–Expensive)*.

SAN VINCENZO (146 A3) (*M E13*)

The seaside resort (pop. 7000) bursts at its seams during summer. It has lovely sandy beaches, great holiday resorts, a yacht marina and a wide selection of leisure activities. A former school that has been converted into an elegant apartment hotel with swimming pool, *Residenza Santa Cecilia* is excellent value for money. (*15*

apartments | Via dell'Asilo 2 | tel. 05 65 70 74 57 | www.santa-cecilia.it | Moderate). Excellent fish dishes are served on the ☀ outdoor terrace with a view of Elba at the *Ristorante La Bitta (daily, in winter closed Mon | Piazza Vittorio Veneto | tel. 05 65 70 40 80 | Moderate–Expensive*.

Giglio Island: Elba's little sister

TUSCAN ARCHIPELAGO (*M A–G 10–19*)

The island of Elba – full of picturesque bays and harbour towns, quaint mountain villages and wooded slopes – is the largest of the islands that make up the Tuscan Archipelago – and is popular with beach-lovers and hiking enthusiasts. The chain also includes Capraia, Giannutri, Giglio, Gorgona, Montecristo and Pianosa.

LUCCA, PISA & VERSILIA

Three provinces in the north-west have shaped the fate of the entire region: charming Lucca (with its lovely Garvagnana countryside), Massa Carrara (between the sea and the Apuan Alps) and Pisa (the former naval superpower) on the alluvial plain of the Arno River mouth. They owe their fortune to the trade along the medieval pilgrimage route, the Via Francigena, which connected France with Rome.

LUCCA

(136 C5) (*∅ E7*) The former city republic, on the left bank of the Serchio, managed

WHERE TO START?
Leave your car at the Carducci car park at the **Porta Sant'Anna**, and start with a stroll on top of the tree-lined city wall. Walking in a clockwise direction you will reach the Porto Santa Maria, where you can descend. Here you will find the tourism office and, a little further to the west, the San Frediano basilica. Take the Via Cavallerizza to the oval Piazza dell' Anfiteatro and a little further south to the watchtower, the Torre Guinigi, which is surrounded by holm oaks.

Photo: Lucca

World famous images: the Leaning Tower of Pisa, Lucca's preserved city walls, marble quarries and the belle époque's bathing culture

to retain its independence until 1847. The city embodies comfort and quality of life and really does have it all: red brick palaces and churches embellished with marble, an old town (closed to traffic) with narrow streets and quiet squares, wonderful restaurants and delicatessens, and elegant fashion boutiques.

The city (pop. 85,000) transformed itself in the Middle Ages into a Renaissance jewel and had a long tradition as a market place for fine cloth. Today Lucca's economy is based on paper production, quality food and tourism.

SIGHTSEEING

LE MURA

This 4km/2.5mi long and 12m/40ft high city wall forms a wide promenade; it has

Carved in marble: sarcophagus of Ilaria del Carretto in Lucca's cathedral

a total of six gates, and was last extended between 1544 and 1645. Today the wall serves as a park where mothers take their children for a stroll, cyclists train and visitors enjoy the views over the city's red rooftops and secret gardens.

MUSEO NAZIONALE PALAZZO MANSI

The museum is housed in a magnificent 16th century city palace that once belonged to a patrician family. There is so much pomp and splendour that the art gallery, with regional art, is almost just a decorative accessory. *Tue–Sat 8.30am–7.30pm | 4 euros | Via Galli Tassi 43*

PIAZZA DELL'ANFITEATRO ★

The houses around the oval piazza in the old town were built on the remains of the original Roman amphitheatre. Sit at one of the outdoor cafés and soak up the atmosphere.

SAN FREDIANO

The church next to the city wall was consecrated in 1147; it has a charming interior with a marble altar (1422) by Jacopo della Quercia and a decorated Romanesque baptismal font. The mosaic on the façade depicts Christ's ascension. *Mon–Sat 8.30am–noon and 3pm–5pm, Sun 10.30am–5pm | Piazza San Frediano*

SAN MARTINO

The greatest treasure of this 12th century cathedral, with its richly decorated Romanesque façade, is the *Volto Santo*, the so-called 'face of Jesus' in the small octagonal temple. The wooden crucifix is venerated as a relic and carried in a procession through the city during September. The marble sarcophagus of Ilaria del Carreto is of great artistic importance, it is a strikingly beautiful piece of work by Jacopo della Quercia that dates back to 1408. *Daily 7am–7pm, winter until 5pm | Piazza San Martino*

SAN MICHELE IN FORO

The citizens built this church, at the former Roman forum, during the 12th century in competition with the cathedral and it remained their meeting place for a long time. The five-storey building has a remarkable marble façade of blind arches with a statue of St Michael on the central portal.

The building is considered one of the most beautiful Romanesque buildings in Tuscany and also has a rich interior by the likes of Andrea della Robbia and Filippino Lippi. *Daily 7.40am–noon and 3pm–6pm | Piazza San Michele*

INSIDER TIP **VILLA CONTRONI-PFANNER**
Built in 1667, a beautiful villa with a garden filled with statues, fountains and secluded corners. *April–Oct daily 10am–6pm | 5.50 euros | Via degli Asili 33*

FOOD & DRINK

ANTICA LOCANDA DELL'ANGELO
The food is some of the best in the city. The ravioli stuffed with duck is amazing! *Closed Sun evening and Mon | Via Pescheria 21 | tel. 05 83 46 77 11 | Moderate–Expensive*

TRATTORIA DA LEO
Popular lunch restaurant serving good, reasonably priced home-style cooking. *Daily | Via Tegrimi 1 | tel. 05 83 49 22 36 | Budget*

ANTICO CAFFÈ DI SIMO
Elegant and historic – during the day they serve coffee and on weekends they also have piano music in the evening. *Closed Mon | Via Fillungo 58*

SHOPPING

ANTICA BOTTEGA DI PROSPERO
Treasure trove of local specialities: olive oil, chestnut flour, spelt and *bazzone*, a spicy ham from the Garfagnana. *Via Santa Lucia 13*

MERCATO DELL'ANTIQUARIATO
Testament of its quality: the antiques market that takes place around the cathedral square every third weekend of the month has been running for 40 years.

INSIDER TIP **TAPPEZZERIA ANGELO SQUALETTI**
Handwoven raw silk and brocade have made the city rich and you can get an idea of the former splendour in this material shop. *Via San Paolino 89*

SPORTS & ACTIVITIES

CYCLING
Experiencing the pedestrian zone of the old town by bicycle is a pleasure, one bike company is: *Cicli Bizzarri (Piazza Santa Maria 32 | tel. 05 83 49 60 31 | www.cicli bizzarri.net | from 2.50 euros/hour or 12.50 euros/day).* The surrounding hilly countryside is better explored on a mountain bike and with an 🙂 eco-guide. Info: *www.eco-guide.it*

⭐ **Campo dei Miracoli in Pisa**
The 'field of miracles' around the Leaning Tower → p. 96

⭐ **Piazza dell'Anfiteatro in Lucca**
So often seen in photographs – the famous oval piazza is unmistakable → p. 86

⭐ **Pietrasanta**
A Mecca for sculptors throughout the ages → p. 94

⭐ **Pontremoli**
Elegant town on the green slopes of the Apennines → p. 95

⭐ **Passeggiata in Viareggio**
An art déco town from the early days of the bathing culture → p. 95

MARCO POLO HIGHLIGHTS

LUCCA

ENTERTAINMENT

VINARKIA
Enjoy tasty snacks *(spuntini)* in this particularly attractive wine bar in a small garden.
Closed Mon | Via Fillungo 188

WHERE TO STAY

ALBERGO CELIDE
Friendly hotel right next to the city wall with individually decorated rooms, its own seafood restaurant and large outdoor terrace. Bicycles available to hotel guests at no charge. *58 rooms | Viale G. Giusti 25 | tel. 05 83 95 41 06 | www.albergocelide.it | Moderate*

SAN LUCA PALACE HOTEL
A carefully renovated hotel in an historic setting, inside the city walls with own garage. *25 rooms | Via San Paolino 103 | tel. 05 83 31 74 46 | www.sanlucapalace.com | Moderate–Expensive*

INFORMATION

Piazza Santa Maria 35 | tel. 05 83 91 99 31 | www.luccaturismo.it

WHERE TO GO

BAGNI DI LUCCA (137 D3) *(ΩΩ F6)*
This dusty little town (pop. 6600, 30km/19mi to the north) was once Europe's most fashionable spa resort. The first casino in Europe opened here (now the tourism office, *Via Umberto 197*) and elegant hotels benefited from the healing powers of the thermal waters. Some of the belle époque villas and spas have since been restored, including the *Terme Bagni di Lucca (daily 7am–12.30pm during the summer also 2.30pm–6pm | Piazza San Martino 11 | www.termebagnidilucca. it)*. Enjoy a sumptuous meal at a reasonable prices in the **INSIDER TIP** *Circolo dei Forestieri (closed Mon | Piazza Jean Verraud 10 | tel. 0 58 38 60 38 | Budget)*.

The beach and nightlife of Camaiore happens down at the beach in the Lido di Camaiore district

BARGA (136 C2) *(Ⓜ E5)*

The breathtaking views of the Apuan Alps from the ☀️ *Piazzale Arringo,* the splendid 12th century *San Cristofano Cathedral* – with the light filtering through the alabaster framed windows onto a 1000 year old figure of Christopher and a marble pulpit supported by lions – all make the 35km/21.5mi trip north to the mountain town (pop. 10,000) well worthwhile. When strolling through the alleyways and steep streets you will be surprised by the beautiful Renaissance buildings which date back to a time when silk production was the centre of the town's existence.

CAMAIORE
(136 B4) *(Ⓜ D6)*

This is quite common: the newer part of the town is located on the seaside with either a yacht marina or a lido and in summer everything centres on tourism. Camaiore is no exception. A friendly family business is the *Hotel dei Tigli (30 rooms | Via Roma 222 | tel. 05 84 61 96 16 | www.hoteldeitigli.it | Moderate).* The old town (pop. 32,000, 25km/15.5mi northwest) is on top of a hill and was constructed in 1255 because Lucca needed an outpost above the Via Aurelia. Camaiore is calm, quiet and peaceful and in the evening tired beach goers stroll through the streets, drink an aperitif, look for souvenirs made by local craftsmen or go to one of the restaurants, like the *Locanda Le Monache (closed Wed | Piazza XXIX Maggio 36 | tel. 05 84 98 92 58 | Expensive).* On the way to the small 9th century Romanesque church *Santo Stefano* in Pieve di Camaiore lies the **INSIDER TIP** wonderful hamlet *Peralta (4 rooms, 7 Apartments | Via Pieve 321 | tel. 05 84 95 12 30 | www.peraltatuscany.com | Moderate)* which has been transformed into individual holiday rentals by a Mexican artist.

GARFAGNANA
(136 B–C 1–2) *(Ⓜ D–E 4–5)*

The soft rolling hills of the Apennines in the east, the craggy mountains of the Apuan Alps in the west and in between pristine valleys, chestnut forests, and picturesque villages: this is the exceptionally beautiful Serchio River valley north of Lucca. The best way to explore it is the gentle way: a hike (there are 110km/68mi of trails) or a walk on a bridle path – signposted *ippovie.*

Start your exploration at Serchio, where valleys lead off to the left and right and where the ruins of castles, small Romanesque churches and deserted monasteries bear witness to a great past. Do try to make a detour to *Borgo a Mozzano* which is dominated by the *Ponte del Diavolo* (Devil's Bridge) and the secluded **INSIDER TIP** *Calomini Hermitage (irregular opening times | tel. 05 83 76 70 20)* that nestles against a towering cliff face. Drive along the left river bank to Gallicano, where the winding SP 39 road starts. At the end of the SP 39 you will also find the stalactite caves, *Grotta del Vento (April–Nov daily Dec–March Mon–Sat 10am–6pm, admission on the hour | 9/14/20 euros depending on the tour | www.grottadelvento.com).* It is a short stretch from Gallicano to *Castel nuovo di Garfagnana* where the fairy-tale castle *Rocca Ariostesca,* with its Renaissance elements, towers above the main town. On Thursday mornings a bustling clothing and vegetable market takes place in the old town where the people from the valley exchange products and gossip.

The Garfagnana is also well known for its gourmet tourism: along the way you will find inviting bars and restaurants that serve regional specialities like **INSIDER TIP** chestnut flour products for instance at the *Osteria Vecchio Mulino (closed Mon | Via Vittorio Emanuele 12 | tel. 0 58 36 21 92 | www.vecchiomulino.com | Moderate)* in

In Massa marble lions guard the Palazzo Cybo Malaspina on the Piazza Aranci

Castelnuovo di Garfagnana and holiday farm houses, that offer their own products, like the *Agriturismo Il Ristoro del Cavaliere (4 apartments | Via Piana | district Cortia | tel. 05 83 60 58 98 | Moderate)* with swimming pool and restaurant at Piazza al Serchio.
Information: *Castelnuovo di Garfagnana | Piazza delle Erbe 1 | tel. 0 58 36 51 69 | www.turismo.garfagnana.eu*

LAGO DI MASSACIUCCOLI
(136 B5) (*ロ D7*)

The shallow lake with its broad band of reeds is a residue of the delta lagoon that was here a few centuries ago. The wetlands are breeding grounds for migratory birds, and form part of the *Parco San Rossore* reserve and can be explored via footpaths and walkways on stilts. On the banks is *Torre del Lago* (pop. 11,000) where the composer Puccini once lived. Today his home is a *museum (summer Tue–Sun 10am–12.40pm and 3pm–6.20pm, winter 10am–12.40pm and 2.30pm–5.10pm |*

7 euros | Belvedere Puccini). His works are performed annually from mid-July until late August during the *Puccini Festival (www.puccinifestival.it)* on an impressive floating stage. During the summer the town is a popular gay meeting spot *(www.friendlyversilia.it).*

VILLE LUCCHESI
(136 C4–5) (*ロ E–F7*)

The splendid country mansions of the patrician families in the surrounding hills here are just as beautiful as those in Lucca. One example is the *Villa Torrigiani (mid March–Oct Mon–Fri 10am–1pm and 3pm–6pm, Sat/Sun 10am–6pm | 10 euros | Via del Gomberaio 3 | www.villelucchesi.net)* in *Camigliano* 10km/6mi east which enchants with its landscaped garden full of grottos, fountains and statues. Another is the *Villa Reale (March–Oct Tue–Sun 10am–1pm and 2pm–6pm | 7 euros | Viale Europa | www.parcovillareale.it)* in *Marlia* 10km/6mi north with its open air boxwood theatre set in a baroque garden.

MASSA

(135 D5) *(m C5–6)* **The Massa Carrara province in the north-west of Tuscany has an idyllic setting: a coast with long sandy beaches, a hinterland with rugged alpine mountains with deep valleys, massive forests and the largest marble mining area in the world.**

The capital Massa (pop. 67,000) relies on a winning formula of sea, marble and Malaspina. Down in the coastal suburb Marina tourism rules, in the old town further up it is craftwork, especially marble, whilst the history of the area is closely linked to the Malaspina family who determined the fate of the city for 350 years.

SIGHTSEEING

INSIDER TIP CASTELLO MALASPINA ≋
In 800 the castle was used as a impenetrable retreat for the city rulers, at its high point it is only accessible via a narrow staircase lane. The view of the city, coast and mountains will take your breath away. The Malaspina family, who lived here since 1442 used the Renaissance castle (15th century) as their stately seat (today it is a museum). *June–Sept daily 10.30am–1pm and 3.30pm–midnight, Oct–May Sun 2.30pm–6.30pm | 5 euros | Via del Forte 15*

PALAZZO CYBO MALASPINA
During the 16th century the Malaspina family had a part of the medieval old town torn down and laid out straight streets. They also built their new residence on the main square. The orange trees along the piazza were planted by Napoleon's sister Elisa Baciocchi, who was the grand duchess of Tuscany during the 19th century. *Piazza degli Aranci*

SANTI PIETRO E FRANCESCO
The cathedral has a beautiful marble façade and double loggias, one on top of each other and its splendid baroque interior houses the Malaspina family tombs. *Daily 9am–7pm | Via Dante*

FOOD & DRINK

BLUE INN
A friendly seafood restaurant in Marina di Massa, ideal for a special evening. *Closed Mon |Via Fortino di San Francesco 9 | tel. 05 85 24 00 60 | Moderate–Expensive*

OSTERIA DEL BORGO
Tasty local dishes like *stordellate* (a type of lasagna), ravioli or stockfish with tomatoes and olives are served in a rustic setting. *Closed Tue | Via Beatrice 17 | tel. 05 85 81 06 80 | Moderate*

SHOPPING

LABORATORIO CERAMICA
In his workshop below the castle the ceramics master Claudio Bonugli combines tradition with artistry. *Via Luigi Staffetti 33*

SPORTS & ACTIVITIES

SAN CARLO TERME
4km/2.5mi out of town the spa offers thermal treatments and a soothing anti-stress programme. *May–Oct | Via dei Colli | tel. 0 58 34 77 03*

ENTERTAINMENT

VESPUCCI 20
The ideal venue for a hip evening in Marina di Massa: first dinner (*Moderate*) on the ≋ terrace with a sea view, then live tango or piano music. *Summer daily, otherwise Thu–Sat | Lungomare di Levante 28*

MASSA

WHERE TO STAY

HOTEL GABRINI
Family run three star hotel on the coast in Marina di Massa. Large garden, 45 comfortable rooms, garage. *Via Luigi Sturzo 19 | tel. 05 85 24 05 05 | www.hotelgabrini.it |* *Moderate*

INFORMATION

Marina di Massa | Lungomare Vespucci 24 | tel. 05 85 24 00 63 | www.apt.massa carrara.it

WHERE TO GO

APUAN ALPS
(135 D–F 4–6) *(ⅅ C–D 5 —6)*
The mountain range rises up to 2000m/ 656ft from the Tyrrhenian Sea. On the coastal side lemon trees bloom during winter, while in the interior snow lingers in the valleys until May. As compensation, rare wild mouflon sheep cavort in the woods and golden eagles nest in the cliffs.

LOW BUDGET

▶ *Incaba (Tue–Sat 9.30am–12.30pm and 3.30pm–7.30pm, Mon 3.30pm– 7.30pm | Via Provinciale 241)* is a wholesale market on the outskirts of Camaiore that sells children's products. Prices are 20 to 40 per cent less than elsewhere in Europe.

▶ The *Outlet D'Avenza (Mon–Fri 10am–1pm and 2.30pm–6.30pm, Sat 9am–12.30pm | Via Aurelia 22)* at the Carrara motorway exit in Avenza sells *alta moda* for men at almost half the price you would pay in the shops.

This is a paradise for hikers, climbers and cavers and the area should not be underestimated. Sturdy shoes are a requirement! In order for the marble mining to be curbed, part of the area has been placed under the protection of the Parco Regionale delle Alpi Apuane *(www.parca puane.it)*. Information can be found in the *Centro Visite (Via San Simon Musico 8 | tel. 0 58 57 99 41)* in Massa and in Castelnuovo di Garfagnana *(Piazza delle Erbe 1 | tel. 05 83 75 73 25)*.

CARRARA (135 D5) *(ⅅ C5)*
This city (pop. 65,000) is synonymous with snow white marble, that is carved in workshops into art *(Carlo Nicoli | on appointment only | Piazza XXVII Aprile 8 | tel. 0 58 57 00 79 | www.nicolisculpture. com)* or souvenirs *(Alberto Danesi | Via Colonnata)*. The charming pedestrian area in the old town is relatively unknown, but there is a lot to discover: the Romanesque *cathedral* with its marble bell tower, the *fountain of Neptune* by Baccio Bandinelli and of course a *marble museum (Mon–Sat 9am–12.30pm and 2.30pm–5pm, during summer 9.30am–1pm and 3.30pm–6pm | 4.50 euros | Viale XX Settembre 85)*.
Enjoy coffee and cake in the *Drogheria Pasticceria Caflisch (Via Roma 2)*, regional dishes in the *Osteria Merope (closed Mon | Via Giuseppe Ulivi 2 | tel. 05 85 77 69 61 | www.osteriamerope.it | Moderate)* and culinary souvenirs in the traditional *Antica Drogheria Riacci (Corso Carlo Rosselli 1)*. Right next door to it you can stay in the best hotel in town, the *Hotel Michelangelo (28 rooms | Corso Carlo Rosselli 3 | tel. 05 85 77 71 61 | www.michelangelocarrara.it | Moderate–Expensive)*.

FORTE DEI MARMI (135 D6) *(ⅅ C6)*
Initially the village with its 100m long jetty was set up to ship blocks of marble. Then came a fortress and fishermen's

houses and – from 1900 – holiday villas for the elite. Today this village (pop. 7800, 10km/6mi to the south) is still a popular destination for well heeled tourists, with

INSIDER TIP LUNIGIANA
(134 B–C 2–4) (*A–B 3–5*)

Endless forests, ruined castles and ancient hamlets – offering culture, hospitality and

Gardens full of flowers, fashionable villas and exclusive beach resorts: this is Forte dei Marmi

a sophisticated and discrete atmosphere, beautiful villas and outrageously expensive beach resorts. The *Hotel Byron (26 rooms | Viale A. Morin 46 | tel. 05 84 78 7 0 52 | www.hotelbyron.net | Expensive)*, in two converted art nouveau villas, has everything to satisfy demanding customers and fits in perfectly.

INSIDER TIP GROTTA ANTRO DEL CORCHIA ● (135 E5) (*D6*)

With 1500 grottos, caves and shafts, the Apuan Alps has more holes than Swiss cheese. Three of the caves (including this one) are open to tourists. This one – in Levigliani di Stazzema on the road from Seravezza to Castelnuovo di Garfagnana – is a giant cave with a labyrinth of tunnels. Two hour guided trips are available. *Variable opening times | 12 euros | Via IV Novembre 70 | www.antrocorchia.it*

excellent cuisine – all make it difficult to understand why this pleasant river valley in the extreme north-west of Tuscany is unknown to so many. The situation was very different during the Middle Ages when thousands of pilgrims, merchants and soldiers passed through here, watched over by almost 100 castles. Few of them are preserved, including the Malaspina family castle in *Fosdinovo (tours Wed Mon 11am, noon, 3.30pm, 4.30pm, 5.30pm, 6.30pm | 6 euros | Via Papiriana 2 | www.castello difosdinovo.it)*. There are many churches along the way that are noteworthy, including the *Pieve di Sorano* on the SS 62 in Filattiera. You can learn more about the area and its people in the *Museo dell' Emigrazione della Gente di Toscana (summer Tue–Sun 9.30am–12.30pm and 4.30pm–7.30pm, winter Sat/Sun 9am– noon and 2pm–5pm | free entrance | www.*

museogenteditoscana.it) in the Castello Lusuolo. The ideal starting point for excursions is the delightful holiday farm with swimming pool, *Podere Conti (9 rooms, 4 apartments | Via Dobbiana Macerie 3 | tel. 34 82 68 18 30 | www.podereconti.com | Moderate)* in Filattiera. More tips visit the website *www.terredilunigiana.com*.

The spicy *lardo di Colonnata* is cured in marble vats

MARBLE QUARRIES IN COLONNATA AND FANTISCRITTI (135 D5) (*ω C5*)

For centuries people have been mining the white 'stone of light' from the mountains above Carrara. An environmental disaster and yet the fascination with the quarry, the *cave*, continues. In Fantiscritti at Miseglia above Carrara *Marmotour (Mon–Fri 11am–5pm, May–Aug until 6.30pm, Sat/Sun 11am–6.30pm | 7 euros | Piazzale Fantiscritti 84 | www.marmotour. com)* organises tours into the impressive underworld. Do not forget your jacket! There is an *open air museum (April–Oct*

daily 9.30am–6.30pm | free entrance | www.cavamuseo.com), where displays of the different marble types and mining and transport methods are exhibited.

A few miles further in Colonnata you can find the much vaunted, delicate bacon *lardo di Colonnata*, at shops like *Marino Giannarelli (Via Comunale di Colonnata 2).* The pork back fat is seasoned and cured in marble vats for months before being delicately sliced. The best restaurant in the region is the *Locandapuana (closed Sun evening and Mon | Via Comunale 1 | tel. 05 85 76 80 17 | www.locandaapuana. com | Budget–Moderate).*

PIETRASANTA ★
(135 E6) (*ω C6*)

The charming fortified town (pop. 25,000, 12km/7.4mi) to the south-east is a Mecca for sculptors and stonemasons. There is one marble workshops after another and you may browse – but only by appointment – one such place is the *Studio Pescarella (tel. 05 84 79 05 76 | www.studio pescarella.com).* Much of the old town is made from marble: its curbstones, benches and the *San Martino Cathedral.* Its brick bell tower is a lovely contrast. It is reached via the Via Garibaldi, past the hotel *Albergo Pietrasanta (Via Garibaldi 35 | tel. 05 84 79 37 26 | www.albergopietrasanta.com | Expensive)*, the delicatessen shop *Antichi Sapori (Via Garibaldi 60)* and the small, but very fine, *Ristorante Zenzero (closed Mon |Via Garibaldi 66 | tel. 38 99 14 68 30 | Moderate)* with excellent fish dishes.

The seaside resort *Marina di Pietrasanta* offers a wide, sandy beach and an intense nightlife. Trendy meeting spots are the jetty at sundown, the dance club *Ostras (Viale Roma 123 | www.ostrasbeach.com)* during weekends and the beach bar during the day. The summer festival *La Versiliana (www.laversilianafestival.it)* adds a necessary dose of culture.

In the hinterland, the village of *Sant'Anna di Stazzema* gained notoriety in 1945 when SS henchmen massacred 540 civilians. The INSIDER TIP *museum (Tue–Sun 3pm–7pm | www.santannadistazzema.org)* commemorates the event.

PONTREMOLI ★
(134 B2) (*Ø A3*)

There is very little hustle and bustle in this elegant little town (pop. 7800) 60km/ 37mi to the north. It has old cafés, like the *Caffè degli Svizzeri (closed Mon | Piazza della Repubblica 21)*, authentic *trattorias* and narrow alleyways and if feels just as it must have in medieval times. It is dominated by the Castello del Piagnaro with the INSIDER TIP *Museo delle Statue Stele Lunigianesi (summer Tue–Sun 9am– 12.30pm and 3pm–6pm, winter 9am–noon and 2pm–5.30pm | 4 euros)* and its prehistoric stone stelae. The town had its heyday as a waypoint along the Via Francigena. Today its wealth lies in the unspoilt nature that surrounds it, medicinal herbs, mushrooms, honey and cheese. In the *Antica Trattoria Pelliccia (closed Tue | Via Garibaldi 137 | tel. 01 87 83 05 77 | Moderate)* they know how to prepare all these treasures. Perfect relaxation in complete seclusion is guaranteed at the *Agriturismo Costa d'Orsola (14 rooms | district Orsola | tel. 01 87 83 33 32 | www.costadorsola.it | Moderate)*.

VERSILIA
(135 D6, 136 A4–5) (*Ø C6–7*)

Endless beaches, with fine sand and shallow water, fringed with shady pine forests: the coastal stretch between Viareggio and Forte dei Marmi is the cradle of the Italian bathing culture that originated here during the mid 19th century. The first to arrive were the Italian upper class and wealthy globetrotters and today Versilia still represents the glamorous modern resort holiday, with all its advantages and disadvantages. During the peak season in July and August the beach is packed cheek by jowl with umbrellas and deck chairs and the road along the beach is one long stretch of fun. There are a wide range of sports and activities to cater to all tastes and hotels and holiday resorts suitable for all budgets. At night you also have a choice between pubs, discos, shopping and outdoor theatre. And there should still be some time left for you to understand just why this little place once became so popular. Information in Viareggio: *Viale Carducci 10 | tel. 05 84 96 22 33 | www.aptversilia.it*

VIAREGGIO (136 A5) (*Ø C–D7*)

Instead of cultural assets the oldest seaside resort in Italy (pop. 64,000, 25km/15.5mi to the south-east) boasts a 3km/1.8mi long 'living room' the ★ *Passeggiata* that runs straight between the pier in the south and the historic hotel Principe di Piemonte. In between are colourful bathing cabins and fine hotels, like the welcoming *Tirrenia (15 rooms | Via San Martino 23 | tel. 05 84 44 96 41 | www.tirreniahotel.it | Moderate)*. There are also some magnificent art nouveau pavilions with cafés (like the unique *Gran Caffè Margherita)*, restaurants and elegant fashion boutiques. The unpretentious restaurant *Romano (closed Mon | Via Giuseppe Mazzini 122 | tel. 05 84 31 382 | Expensive)*, is one of the best seafood restaurants. In the tourist port *La Madonnina* marine biologists organise ● INSIDER TIP sailing trips for whale and dolphin watching *(summer daily, winter Sat/Sun 9.30am–5pm | 70 euros incl. lunch | by reservation only at tel. 33 56 56 44 69 or cetus@supereva.it)*. For those visiting during the winter, you should not miss Viareggio's famous carnival parade with satirical papier mâché floats *(www.viareggio.ilcarnevale.com)*.

CITY **WHERE TO START?**
At the **Campo dei Miracoli** (field of wonders) of course! You will need to leave your car outside of the city gates, in a car park like the one on Via San Cammeo 5 at the west gate. It costs 2 euros per hour, but it will save you time. From Piazza dei Miracoli take the Via Santa Maria and Via dei Mille to the central square, the Piazza dei Cavalieri. From there the Via Ulisse Dini leads up to Borgo Stretto, the arcaded shopping street, which ends at the Ponte di Mezzo. To the right, on the other bank of the River Arno, is the quaint little Santa Maria della Spina church.

PISA

MAP ON PAGE 98

(140 B2) *(Ø D8)* **Every year millions of tourists come to Pisa (pop. 88,000) to admire its famous landmarks, and make the mistake of ignoring the rest of the city. But this lively student city has a lot more to offer: magnificent monuments, tranquil gardens, inviting squares, arcaded streets and elegant shops. The key to understanding Pisa's splendour lies in the Middle Ages: back then this former maritime republic's fleet dominated the Mediterranean Sea and could increase their wealth without unhindered.**

SIGHTSEEING

CAMPO DEI MIRACOLI ★

The 'field of miracles' with its four monuments made from bright white Carrara marble – cathedral, baptistery, bell tower

and monumental cemetery – is situated at the western gate of the medieval city walls. During construction it was evident that the alluvial land was not the best to build on. The 56m/184ft high *Leaning Tower (April–Sept daily 8.30am–8pm, Oct and March 9am–5.30pm, Nov and Feb 9.30am–5.30pm, Dec/Jan 10am–4.30pm | no children under 8 years | 15 euros | advanced booking (17 euros) at www.opapisa.it is advisable due to the limited number of visitors allowed)*, is clear evidence of this. Shortly after construction started in 1173, the earth started to give way and the builders tried in vain to compensate for the lean. They have now managed to stop it from sinking any further. The *Cathedral (April–Sept daily 10am–8pm, Oct and March 10am–6pm, Nov–Feb 10am–12.45pm and 2–5pm | 2 euros, Nov–Feb free)* which was consecrated in 1118, is in the form of a Latin cross, and is a masterpiece of the Pisan Romanesque architecture. The façade (with its four galleries of elegant marble columns), the front and rear bronze doors (decorated with scenes from the New Testament) and the oval dome – are all truly spectacular. The interior is decorated with Byzantine mosaics. Also remarkable are the two-tone pointed arches that run through both sides of the nave, the Gothic pulpit by Giovanni Pisano (1301–11) with scenic reliefs, the tomb of the German Emperor Heinrich VII as well as the bronze chandelier that supposedly helped Galileo Galilei discover the law of the pendulum.

The façade of the 1152 *Baptistery (April–Sept daily 8am–8pm, Oct and March 9am–6pm, Nov–Feb 10am–5pm | 5 euros)* has the same blind arches and galleries as the cathedral. Its splendid interior houses a baptismal font from 1246, an altar with the inlay work and a hexagonal pulpit by Nicola Pisano which is one of the first examples of Gothic sculpture in

Italy. The marble ensemble is completed on the green lawns of the *Camposanto (April–Sept daily 8am–8pm, Oct and March 9am–6pm, Nov–Feb 10am–5pm | 5 euros)*, or the Monumental Cemetery that is enclosed within four porticoes. The late antiquity sarcophagi were initially set up around the cathedral and were used as tombs. The wall frescoes were damaged during World War II. The fresco cycle of Buonamico Buffalmacco from the 14th century with the episodes The Triumph of Death, Last Judgement and The Hell, were preserved. If you prefer to visit more museums, opt for the cheaper multi-ticket *(www.opapisa.it)*.

MURALE DI PISA

Here the city shows that it is not stuck in history: in 1989 Keith Haring was commissioned to paint the wall of the Convento Sant'Antonio at the train station. The resulting mural is typical of his unique line drawings. *Piazza Vittorio Emanuele II*

MUSEO NAZIONALE SAN MATTEO

The former Benedictine monastery on the banks of the Arno houses more than 200 panels of the Pisa School, painted wooden crosses and a triptych (1321) by Simone Martini. *Tue–Sat 8.30am–7pm, Sun 8.30am–1pm | 5 euros | Piazza San Matteo in Soarta 1*

ORTO BOTANICO

A wonderful place to take a breather! The botanical garden, one of the oldest in the world was established in 1543 in order for the medical faculty to have medicinal plants for educational purposes. *Mon–Sat 8.30am–1pm | 2.50 euros | V. Luca Ghini 5*

PIAZZA DEI CAVALIERI

Seven streets lead into this stately square, which was the centre of secular power during the Middle Ages. The *Palazzo dei Cavalieri* – which is decorated with sgraffito paintings and is very impressive – was radically redesigned in 1562 by Giorgio Vasari and today is the seat of the Scuolo

The most famous detail in Pisa's cathedral: the octagonal Gothic pulpit by Giovanni Pisano

Normale Superiore. The *Palazzo dell' Orologio* (clock palace) was built next to it in 1605 using two dilapidated towers, including the 'hunger tower' where a city governor was imprisoned and starved to death in 1288.

SANTA MARIA DELLA SPINA

This small stone church was built in 1230 on the edge of the Arno as a shrine for a thorn (spina) from Christ's crown. It was extended in the 14th century and in 1871, when it was threatened by the rising Arno, dismantled and moved to higher ground. The building with its statues, small pointed turrets and gables is a superb example of Gothic architecture. *June–Aug daily 10am–1pm and 3pm–6pm, Sept–May Tue–Fri 10am–2pm, Sat/Sun 10am–2pm and 3pm–5pm | Lungarno Gambacorti*

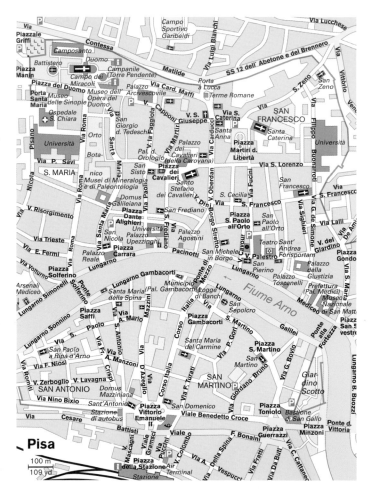

Pisa

100 m
109 yd

FOOD & DRINK

CAGLIOSTRO

A contemporary interior inside old walls, serving modern variations of traditional dishes. Some evenings also outside on the square when the weather is good. *Closed Tue | Via del Castelletto 26 | tel. 0 50 57 54 13 | Moderate–Expensive*

ANTICA TRATTORIA IL CAMPANO

Popular meeting spot for the locals, in the maze of the old town, that serves Tuscan dishes. *Closed Thu afternoons and Wed | Via Cavalca 19 | tel. 0 50 58 05 85 | www. ilcampano.com | Budget–Moderate*

OSTERIA DEI CAVALIERI

Wonderful atmosphere and tasty dishes, centrally positioned halfway between Campo dei Miracoli and the Piazza dei Cavalieri. *Closed Sat afternoons and Sun | Via San Frediano 16 | tel. 0 50 58 08 58 | www.osteriacavalieri.pisa.it | Moderate*

SHOPPING

MERCATO DELLE VETTOVAGLIE

The food market, on the Piazza delle Vetto-vaglie with its ochre yellow houses, is an institution. *Mon–Sat mornings | Piazza delle Vettovaglie*

PASTICCERIA SALZA

There are lots of elegant speciality shops on the Borgo Stretto and the sweet temptations in the traditional bakery at no. 46 are a must. *Closed Mon.*

SPORTS & ACTIVITIES

BICYCLES

Bicycles are the best mode of transport in the narrow, medieval streets and along the banks of the Arno River. Tandems, Segways and bicycle rickshaws are also available. *From 4 euros/hour | Via Uguccione della Faggiola 41 | tel. 0 50 56 18 39 | www.eco voyager.it*

Experience a classic Mediterranean food market at the Mercato delle Vettovaglie

From March to October, city guides organise a two hour introductory tour through the centre and on Monday and Saturday they are conducted in English. *Meeting place 10.45am Piazza XX Settembre | 12 euros*

The sleek cult scooter has its own museum in Pondera

ENTERTAINMENT

INSIDER TIP SUNSET CAFÉ
Beach bar in Marina di Pisa (15km/9mi). Drinks and snacks are served on the beach and on weekends jazz or DJ music. *Summer daily 6pm–2am | Via Litoranea 40 a (opposite Camping Internazionale) | www.sunset-cafe.it*

TEATRO SANT'ANDREA
A decommissioned church now used as a cultural space for theatre, concerts and dance. *Via del Cuore | tel. 0 50 54 23 64 | www.teatrosantandrea.it*

WHERE TO STAY

ROYAL VICTORIA
Simple yet endearing mid range hotel in a renovated city palace on the Arno embankment. With roof terrace and garage. *48 rooms | Lungarno Pacinotti 12 | tel. 0 50 94 01 11 | www.royalvictoria.it | Budget–Moderate*

VILLA DI CORLIANO
This charming guest house in a somewhat run-down baroque villa (11km/7mi north in Rigoli) has its own park. Although the eleven rooms are simply furnished that is offset by the fresco painted common room. *Via Statale Abetone 50 | tel. 0 50 81 81 93 | www.villacorliano.it | Moderate*

INFORMATION

Piazza Vittorio Emanuele II 16 | tel. 05 04 22 91; Piazza XX Settembre | tel. 0 50 91 09 33 | www.pisa.turismo.toscana.it

WHERE TO GO

INSIDER TIP BASILICA SAN PIERO A GRADO (140 A2) (*∅ D8*)
5km/3mi to the west is this 11th century triple-naved basilica, which is said to have been built where Peter first set foot on Italian soil. The walls of the central nave are decorated with wonderful frescoes. Beneath the 14th century altar canopy are the remains of the original church and a Roman building. *Daily 8am–7pm, in the summer until 8pm | Via Vecchia di Marina 5*

CERTOSA DI PISA
(140 C2) (*∅ E8*)
10km/6mi to the east, on the slopes of the Pisa mountains is Calci and one of the largest monasteries in Tuscany. A part of the 14th century Carthusian monastery is

now used as a museum for natural and local history. The section that displays fresh water fish from all over the world is remarkable. *Tue–Sat 8.30am–6.30pm, Sun 8.30am–12.30pm | 4 euros | Via Roma 79*

PARCO REGIONALE DI MIGLIARINO, SAN ROSSORE, MASSACIUCCOLI
(136 A–B 5–6, 140 A–B 1–3) (*Ⓜ D7–9*)
This nature reserve on the outskirts of Pisa is a mosaic of different ecological systems that stretches over 88 square miles along the coast between Livorno and Viareggio. Especially popular is the section of the former royal estate Tenuta di San Rossore, a marshland with pine trees, scrub and wetlands in the estuary between the Arno and the Serchio. You can explore it on foot, bicycle, horseback or carriage. The starting point is the guesthouse *La Sterpaia*, where you can get brochures and park products. The signposted *entrance to the park (summer daily 8am–7pm, winter*

8am–5.30pm | free entrance) at the end of the Viale delle Cascine can be reached from the Via Aurelia (SS 1). Most of the park area is only accessible upon payment of a fee. Information and reservations in the visitors' centre *Centro Visite San Rossore (Cascine Vecchie | tel. 0 50 53 01 01 | www. parcosanrossore.org)*.

PONTEDERA
(141 D2) (*Ⓜ F8*)
The Vespa, the legendary scooter from Pontedera (25km/15.5mieast), is synonymous with the Italian way of life. Original models on display in the workshop museum ● *Museo Piaggio (Tue–Sat 10am–6pm | free entrance | Viale R. Piaggio 7 | www.museopiaggio.it)* documents its success. 15km/9mi further south-east is the *Borgo di Colleoli Resort (65 apartments and 12 rooms | Via San Bartolomeo 6 | tel. 05 87 62 25 24 | www.borgocolleoli.com | Moderate)* in a lovingly restored Tuscan hamlet.

BOOKS & FILMS

▶ **Life Is Beautiful (La vita è bella)** – a 1997 film that tells the story of a Jewish family from Arezzo in an Italian concentration camp during World War II. Directed by Roberto Benigni (who also plays the lead) it is about a father who tries to distract his young son from the horrors of the war with imaginative stories.

▶ **Under the Tuscan Sun** – An enchanting memoir by Frances Mayes (1996) that recounts the author's adventures of buying and restoring an abandoned villa in the Tuscan countryside. It has all the elements of a great Italian travel

story and was also made into a romantic comedy drama (2003) starring Diane Lane and directed by Audrey Wells.

▶ **A Death in Tuscany** – A novel by insider Michele Giuttari (first published in English 2008) who is the former chief of police for Florence. His insights into the reality of Italian police work make this crime novel all the more compelling.

▶ **Hannibal** – Starring Anthony Hopkins as Hannibal Lecter, who works in the library of the Palazzo Vecchio, director Ridley Scott's sequel (2000) to 'The Silence of the Lambs' is set in Florence.

TRIPS & TOURS

The tours are marked in green in the road atlas, the pull-out map and on the back cover

1 ON THE TRAIL OF PIERO DELLA FRANCESCA

Painting was his vocation, but mathematic his passion: the Tuscan Piero della Francesca (1420–92) attached great importance to the strict geometric structure of his paintings as well as to the natural representation of his figures, landscapes and light. This revolutionised art. Some of his important works are in Arezzo, in his hometown Sancepolcro and in Monterchi, the birthplace of his mother. For this trip we follow in his footsteps you will need to set aside a whole day,

even though the journey is only 90km/ 50mi long.

Start in Arezzo. Leave the car in the car park at the Piazza del Popolo and from there go along the Via Andrea Cisalpino to the cathedral → p. 54. In the left side nave, next to the door to the sacristy, his elegant and graceful Maria Magdalena looks down from above.

At about the halfway point on the way back is the San Francesco basilica → p. 55 where the artist created one of the most beautiful frescoes in European art history, the ten part series 'Legend of the Holy Cross'. He spent nearly a decade on the 980 ft2 fresco and changed the setting

---

Photo: Vineyards at Greve in Chianti

Criss-cross Tuscany: by car to Piero della Francesca, by bicycle through Chianti and on foot in the Apuan Alps

from the Holy Land to Tuscany: Arezzo became Jerusalem, and the Tuscan countryside became the biblical fields and the Queen of Sheba became a Renaissance noblewoman.

The next stop is the village of **Monterchi** with the painting **Madonna del Parto**. Take the SS 73 on the outskirts of Arezzo towards Sansepolcro. Shortly after the four-lane section of the road comes to an end, the road in Le Ville turns to the right and leads to the village which is then a further 3km/1.8mi away. On a hill below the medieval village centre a signpost points the way to the **museum** (daily 9am–1pm and 2pm–7pm, winter until 5pm | 3.50 euros | Via Reglia 1) at the town wall. It was built especially to house the Madonna, a painting that depicts her flanked by two protective angels and which seems to show the Tuscan peasant country life. It was originally located in the cemetery chapel on the town's outskirts and women prayed in front of it for children. It was the first time ever that the Madonna was depicted as a pregnant woman. 'Immoral!' railed the church. They wanted Mary to always be depicted as an immortal virgin and not as an earthly being. It is believed that this is the reason why one of the most brilliant artists of the early Renaissance was literally hushed up until the 20th century. From the rear windows of the museum you can look out over exactly the same landscape with its rows of cypress trees, hamlets and rivers that appear again and again in his paintings. If you arrive in Monterchi at lunchtime you can spend the time – until the museum opens in the afternoon – enjoying Tuscan lunch in the *Vecchia Osteria* on the left of the museum. *Closed Tue | Via dell'Ospedale 16 | tel. 0 57 57 01 21 | Budget–Moderate*

The last stop is 11km/7mi away, **Sansepolcro → p. 59**, Piero della Francesca's birthplace. At the northern outskirts of Monterchi take a right turn and follow the SS 73 keeping an eye out for the signpost 'Centro' after the motorway bridge. There is free parking at the tree-lined Viale Armando Diaz. In front of the city wall go left up to the Via Aggiunti and turn right. The town museum is at no. 65 **Museo Civico** *(summer daily 9.30am–1.30pm and 2.30pm–7pm, winter 9.30am–1pm and 2.30pm–6pm | 6 euros)* with four paintings by the artist: the 'La Madonna della Misecordia' and three murals including 'La Resurrenzione', said by the writer Aldous Huxley to be the most beautiful Renaissance painting of all. In the fresco the Son of God emerges from his tomb, unnoticed by the guards. The diagonal layout shows the background in depth, and in the foreground the figures are very

vivid because of the artist's clever use of light.

Next to the museum is the town's medieval centre. On the left along the Via della Fonte you will reach the **home of the painter**. After a devastating fire, only the stairs and a fountain at the entrance remain of the original building. If you still have some time, walk through the pretty town centre and enjoy the comfortable pace of this small town with its many shops and cosy pubs. Schedule an hour for the return trip to Arezzo.

2 HIKING IN THE MARBLE MOUNTAINS ☺

Throughout the world the name Carrara is synonymous with marble, the coveted white stone. There is hardly a country that does not have at least a monument or hotel foyer made from the white stone mined in the Apuan Alps since the time of the Romans. Artists such as Michelangelo got his material for his sculptures from the northwest of Tuscany. But few people know that the rocky karst mountains that reach almost 2000m/6561ft into the sky, are also a paradise for hikers. A daytrip from Carrara to Monte Sagro is enough to see the impressive landscape – its summits, deep valleys and endless forests – with new eyes. You will need sturdy footwear, sun and rain protection, food, water and some mountaineering experience. The final section is very steep!

If you are not holidaying in the vicinity, travel to **Carrara → p. 92** the day before and stay at the pleasant bed & breakfast *Antica Carrara (5 rooms | Via dell'Arancio 17 | tel. 0 58 57 42 75 | Budget)* in the traffic-free old town centre. From there it is 15 minutes to the bus terminal, where the blue line 39 country bus leaves at 8am for Campo Cecine *(www.catspa.it)*. After about an hour the bus stops at **Rifugio Carrara** at 1320m/4330ft, the starting point of the hike. You can get *panini* and pasta in the Alpine Club mountain huts – they are open all year long. If you come back too late, you can even stay here overnight in simple four-bed rooms – own sleeping bag a prerequisite.

In the valley between Monte Borla and Monte Sagro the first stone bridge appears. Continuing on this level in a southerly direction you will reach the pass ☀ **Foce di Pianza** (1289 m/4229ft) where a marble road is used by trucks to transport the heavy blocks into the valley, you can also drive up here by car.

The quarries in Colonnata provided Michelangelo with his marble

The easy, popular hike to the summit of Monte Sagra takes about four hours with an altitude change of 500m/1640ft. The hiking route 173 takes you across an alpine meadow past the remains of ancient shepherd dwellings in a shady beech forest. On the northern side of Monte Borla you will get to a ☀ boulder field. Here you can enjoy a postcard panorama of the mountain landscape of Lunigiana in the north dominated by the stone cathedral of Pizzo d'Uccello.

A lot of tourists like to drive up as this means they will have time for a dip in the ocean afterwards. Up here, the Gulf of La Spezia and the largest marble mining area in the world lies at your feet. In the Carrara hinterland alone there are some 85 quarries in operation and 185 in total in the Apuan Alps. From afar, some of them look like rock castles, others look like a cubist arenas. Earlier the rock was cut out of the mountain with wire ropes. Sand and water were necessary for this, which explains the many rusty tanks that lie around.

From the Foce di Pianza pass you proceed on the 172 hiking trail, first over a wide ridge and then left along the slope. There you can see some trenches, remnants of the German defensive Gothic Line from World War II. Half an hour later you will reach the **Foce della Faggiola** pass (1464 m/4803ft). From up here you will look down on the marble village Colonnata. Today the name is especially associated with the delicious lard that is cured here in marble vats. This is also the village that supplied Michelangelo with his marble.

The last leg to the summit of **Monte Sagro** at 1750m/5741ft is marked in blue. Initially the route takes you across a treeless hillside meadow, behind the north-west side it becomes steeper. As a reward you will be able to see from the ☀ viewing platform, to the west the ocean and to the east the endless vistas of rock and forest, with small villages dotted here and there. The village directly below is Vinca where German SS soldiers staged a revenge campaign in 1944.

The return trip is the same way as far as the Pianza mountain pass. Instead of walking to your right back through the beech forest to the mountain hut, you can walk approx. 2km/1.2mi on the broad marble road. Then a narrow forest trail turns off to the right that takes you back to **Rifugio Carrara**. From its ☀ terrace you can see Corsica if the weather is good.

3 A TWO-WHEEL RIDE THROUGH THE BACK ROADS OF CHIANTI

Strade bianche ('white' or un-surfaced roads) are as much a part of Tuscany as art, cypresses and red wine. For centuries the dusty roads were the only connection between remote villages, castles and wine estates. They led over hills and were flanked by cypresses so that people could see from afar.

As recently as 20 years ago you could travel from Florence for 500km/310mi without touching tarmac. Although that is no longer possible there are still many *strade bianche* and it is on these back roads that you can travel into the soul of Tuscany, the landscape that has lost touch with time. They force you to go slow, and to experience the balance and harmony of this landscape that has been so shaped by man. It is easy to drive on them with any type of vehicle (when renting a car, check the rental terms!) but the best option by far is to choose a Vespa or mountain bike. This way the experience will be far more intense, the play of light on the hills or the smell of the surrounding countryside. No matter how you travel, take along a picnic basket and do not forget water, sun protection and a road map in scale 1 : 25,000.

A highlight for those who love scenic landscape is the 20km/12mi long stretch from Panzano to the wine estate Castello di Volpaia and to Radda in Chianti. To the left and right, the perfect Tuscan mosaic – lines of dead straight vines, silver shimmering olive trees majestic cypress avenues, medieval farms and small oak forests – as far as the eye can see. In **Panzano**, first make a short detour to the little church **Pieve San Leolino** on the village border. From the Strada Chiantigiana (SS 222) after about 1km turn left after the village. The Romanesque building with its picturesque cloister was a stopover for pilgrims and believers during the Middle Ages. Just before it is a typical Tuscan hotel, an ancient villa set in a park, that promises luxury and comfort **Villa Le Barone** *(29 rooms | Via San Leolino 19 | tel. 0 55 85 26 21 | www.villalebarone.com | Expensive)*.

Stay on the narrow road towards the north until you reach a crossroad, where you can turn left to Panzano. Here you take the road to the right to Montemaggio; it turns into a gravel road after a few meters. Now there is no way you can get

roof ensemble of **Castello di Volpaia** *(tel. 05 77 73 80 66 | www.volpaia.com | Expensive)* appears in the distance. It is a fortified wine estate that dates back to the

Castello di Volpaia in Chianti: a picturesque fortified village that is a must

lost. Simply follow the white signs to the Castello di Volpaia. Initially the roads are lined with cypresses. Then the landscape becomes wild, the undergrowth thick and mighty oaks and massive rocks line the way. Alternating to the left and right the hilly landscape opens up and you can see to the horizon on both sides. Chestnut trees alternate with spruce and beeches and during spring, lots of yellow broom.

At the halfway mark you will find a shady rest area under high trees, where you can pause and soak up the nature. As soon as the cypresses start to get more frequent you are almost at the final destination. Just after a narrow curve, the charming

11th century and the owners have carefully restored the almost perfectly preserved medieval castle village, the houses, churches and towers and given them a new life. On the small village square is the former church where you can get *panini*, both restaurants serve delicious Tuscan dishes and wine and olive oil from the estate are sold in the *enoteca*.

If you want to enjoy the magic of the old walls for longer, you will also find five holiday apartments with a swimming pool, a cooking school and a manicured rose garden. A paved road leads from the village square further on to **Radda in Chianti → p. 65** and thus back into the present day.

SPORTS & ACTIVITIES

In Tuscany many people are devoted to sport and visiting holidaymakers also benefit from the extensive leisure activities on offer. An active holiday is the ideal accompaniment to pasta, wine and culture.

CREATIVE

The Tuscan landscape – blessed with culture and nature – is the perfect setting in which to unleash your hidden talents, or it can also be the ideal place for meditation and self-discovery. Initially only secluded farms offered privately organised workshops, but today even renowned academies and smaller tour operators offer creative courses – with all the comforts – for people who have a need for spirituality or need to de-stress. The workshops range from writing to sculpting, painting, pottery, music, tango lessons, Nordic walking or meditative star gazing.

There are also courses about 🕙 biodynamic and organic farming *(www.wwoof.it/en)* as well as the more traditional language courses with Italian lessons for beginners through to advanced that have more recently been combined with fashion or wine workshops, studio visits and cooking courses.

Photo: Maremma near the mouth of the Ombrone

In Tuscany you can be sporty – on a bicycle or on horseback – or relax in the spas and thermal baths of the health resorts

CYCLING

Cycling is a popular sport in the region. During weekends, there are throngs of cyclists on the roads and as the conditions are often hilly and steep with winding country tracks, they are also ideal for the more ambitious cyclists. The same goes for mountain bikers that can often be seen on the high plateaus of the Apuan Alps, the Apennines or on Monte Amiata, not always to the delight of conservationists. Many communities have responded to the growing demand and offer cycling-themed packages on their websites. The province of Siena and Mugello are especially active. See *www.terresiena.it* and *www.mugellotoscana.it* for information about bicycle rentals and cyclist-friendly accommodation. A curiosity is the historic cycling race *Eroica (www.eroica-ciclismo.it)* during the autumn in Chianti. Anyone can participate – provided that there is still a place left – and provided that you use a bicycle that is more than 20 years old and dress in clothing from yesteryear.

GOLF

The English imported the game and in 1889 the first course was laid out in Florence. Since then the number of certi-

HIKING

Tuscany is Italy's most densely wooded region and has exceptional trails, even by Europe's high standards. It is not surprising then that it is covered in a dense network of themed trails that are generally well maintained and clearly marked. The ideal hiking time is from mid April to mid June and then again in September and October. On weekends you will be sharing the trails with the many Italians who love

The superb mountain vista of the steep and rugged Apuan Alps

fied courses between the coast and the Apennines have grown to 16. A handicap of 36 is required. Many of the beautifully landscaped courses are open all year round, especially those that are close to the coast and have the benefit of a mild climate. A very informative website, but unfortunately only in Italian, is *www.toscanagolf.it.*

hiking. During the week, however, you may often have the trails all to yourself. Many routes have holiday farms, bed & breakfast or eco-accommodation along the way. In almost every Pro Loco tourist information office you can get free detailed maps and on the website at *www. turismo.intoscana.it* (choose the English language option and the 'trekking' in the search tab). There is also a *Walking Festival (www.tuscanywalkingfestival.it)* with many events organised throughout the region from mid-April to November.

HORSEBACK RIDING

The Maremma region is well known as a riding paradise, the appropriate infrastructure is in place because traditionally the cattle in the Maremma nature reserve are herded on horseback and experienced riders can accompany the Tuscan cowboys, the *butteri,* by appointment *(Azienda Agricola Alberese | www.alberese.com).* But there are also plenty of other areas of untouched nature such as in Garfagnana, in Casentino or in the Orcia Valley where there are *ippovie* – horse trails – scenic routes with cultural and culinary experiences. In many places holiday farms offer multi-day riding treks. They provide the horses and organise meals and accommodation. The Turismo Equestro ensures high standards and is marked by the symbol of a green horse's head against a red background. The most common routes and addresses can be found at *www.turismo. intoscana.it* (choose the English language option and the 'Horseback Tourism' tab).

TUSCANY UNDERGROUND

Speleologists have always known that Tuscany is as beautiful and varied on the inside as it is on the outside. In the Apennines and the Apuan Alps, there is a 270km/168mi long network of around 1500 underground passages, caves and stalactite caves and many of them are open to the public. There are also a large number of abandoned mines where – until the 1970s – pyrite, iron ore and mercury was mined. Some have been converted into mining museums. And finally,

some municipalities allow you to take a look into their inner workings and have opened their INSIDER TIP medieval irrigation system for viewing, for instance the *I Bottini* in Siena. For more information about Siena's urban underground waterways exploration see *www.turismo.intoscana.it* (choose the English language option and the 'Underground Tuscany' tab).

WATER SPORTS

Along the coast, water sports fans have endless array of possibilities. Boat owners can drop anchor in one of the various large or small ports as well as in the natural bays. There are ideal conditions for scuba divers on the rocky Monte Argentario coast in front of the Piombino foothills or along the coast of Vada, south of Livorno. There are dive centres in Porto Santo Stefano, Piombino and Livorno. The wind along the coast of the Tyrrhenian Sea is also perfect for surfers and sailors. And you can book a sailing trip with a skipper to the island archipelago for whale and dolphin watching. Information: *www.costadeglietruschi.it* tab: *sport and recreation* then *sail and windsurf.*

WELLNESS & SPAS

Thermal water to treat the body and soul was something that even the Romans enjoyed in Tuscany. During the 18th century these healing waters developed into elegant resorts like Montecatini Terme or Bagni di Lucca. The current term of spa has developed into a veritable wellness industry over the past few years, from the curative water spa Equi Terme in the Apuan Alps, to the hot springs of San Casciano dei Bagni on the border, to Lazio to the private beauty spa Villa Ferraia near Siena. You can get a good overview at *www.turismo.intoscana.it* tab 'Spas'.

TRAVEL WITH KIDS

Children love a beach holiday and Tuscany, with its long sandy beaches and shady pine groves, is perfect. On the coast here are numerous blue flag beaches while in the interior there are medieval villages behind every hill that could have come straight out of the Inkheart series or the Twilight saga.

FLORENCE & THE NORTH

MUSEO CON PERSONAGGI IN MOVIMENTO IN SCARPERIA
(139 D3) *(ᗑ K6)*
Tinkers, basket weavers and cheese makers are only three of the 70 movable wooden figures that demonstrate everyday life in a typical Tuscan village during the first half of the 20th century. The museum's creator, Falerio Lepri, shows his little works of art work on *Sundays by appointment (summer 3.30pm–6.30pm, winter 3pm–6pm). District Sant'Agata | Via Montaccianico | tel. 05 58 40 67 50*

MUSEO STIBBERT IN FLORENCE ●
(138 C5) *(ᗑ J–K7)*
A chamber of wonders! In the 19th century the eccentric Englishman, Frederick Stibbert, began collecting curiosities and filled his massive villa with souvenirs and unusual objects from around the world.

Photo: Giardino dei Tarocchi

Lots of opportunity for fun and games: there is always something for children to do in Tuscany

The fairy tale castle is situated in a beautiful park (ideal for a picnic) and is easily reached with the no. 4 bus from the train station. *Museum Mon–Wed 10am–2pm, Fri–Sun 10am–6pm, guided tour every hour on the hour, park daily 8am–7pm, winter until 5pm | museum 6 euros, children under 12 years 4 euros, free admission to park | Via Federigo Stibbert 26 | www. museostibbert.it*

PARCO DI PINOCCHIO IN COLLODI
(137 D4) (*∅ F7*)

A whisper path, a fairy cloud and a Venetian lagoon carousel: the theme park in the home town of Pinocchio's inventor Carlo Lorenzini, is full of surprises. In the wonderful baroque gardens of the Villa Garzoni (Piazza della Vittoria 1) next door, is butterfly house. *March–Oct daily 8.30am, Nov–Feb 9am-sunset | combi-ticket 20 euros,*

The colourful markets attract young fashionistas

children (3–14 years) 16 euros | Via San Gennaro 3 | www.pinocchio.it

PARCO IL GIGANTE IN VAGLIA
(136 C4) (*∅ J6–7*)
Skate, climb or swing through trees on seven different courses in this adventure park. Three hours of fun are guaranteed, every extra hour is 5 euros. Helmet and climbing harness included in the price. *June–Sept daily, Oct/Nov and March–May Sat/Sun 9.30am–7pm | 18 euros, children (8–12 years) 14 euros, under 8 years 10 euros | Via Fiorentina 276 | www.alberovivo.it*

AREZZO, SIENA & CHIANTI

BAMBIMUS – MUSEO D'ARTE PER BAMBINI IN SIENA (143 D6) (*∅ K11*)
The children's museum in Siena has temporary exhibitions and workshops especially designed for children. They also have a permanent exhibition of drawings by children from all over the world. *Daily 10.30am–6.30pm | 6 euros, children under 11 free | Complesso Museale Santa Maria della Scala | Piazza del Duomo 2 | www.comune.siena.it/bambimus*

PARCO PREISTORICO IN PECCIOLI
(141 E3) (*∅ F9*)
This park between Pontedera and Volterra has 20 life-size dinosaurs and other prehistoric animals on display. Playground and lawn for picnics. *Daily 9am–7pm, winter 9am–6pm | 4 euros, children under 3 free | Via dei Cappuccini | www.parco preistorico.it*

MAREMMA & COSTA DEGLI ETRUSCHI

IL GIARDINO DEI TAROCCHI
(151 E4) (*∅ L18*)
The larger than life, colourful objects are not just for looking at. Children are allowed to peek inside or climb on top. *April–mid Oct daily 2.30pm–7.30pm, Nov–March 1st Sat of the month 9am–1pm | 10,50 euros, Nov–March free, children (6–18 years) 6 euros, under 6 years free | www.nikide saintphalle.com*

PARCO ACQUA VILLAGE IN CECINA
MARE (140 C6) (*ⓜ E11*)
Giant slides, Jacuzzi lagoon, wave pool, beach volleyball and a baby club: holiday fun is guaranteed. Almost 60km/37mi to the south in Follonica, district Mezzaluna is a second water park with similar facilities. *Mid June–mid Sept daily 10am–6pm | 20 euros, after 3pm 14 euros, Sun 22 euros, children (3–11 years) 15 euros, after 3pm 10 euros | Via Tevere 25 | www.acquavillage.it*

PARCO CAVALLINO MATTO IN MARINA
DI CASTAGNETO ☺ (146 A2) (*ⓜ E12*)
An ecologically sustainable fun park with miniature railways, mini golf and jumping castles for the little ones and roller coaster, white water route and quad bike trail for the older ones, they also have a nature and eco-trail. *April–mid May and mid Sept–Oct Sat/Sun, mid May–mid Sept daily 10am–6pm | 20 euros, children under 10 years 16 euros, under 90cm/34inches free | Via Po 1 | www.cavallinomatto.it*

PARCO CIELO VERDE IN MARINA DI
GROSSETO (150 A1) (*ⓜ H16*)
Long, wide beaches, easy cycle paths and clean water are exactly why this coastal suburb of Grosseto got the 'child-friendly' label. It is also no coincidence that the Florentine adventure park, Il Gigante, has a branch in the camping village Cieloverde during summer. *Mid June–mid Sept daily, mid May–mid June and mid Sept–mid Oct Sat/Sun 10am–7.30pm | 18 euros, children (6–14 years) 14 euros and 10 euros (3–6 years) | Via della Trappola 180 | www.alberovivo.it*

INSIDER TIP ▶ PARCO ARCHEO-
MINERARIO DI SAN SILVESTRO
(146 B3) (*ⓜ F13*)
Visitors can today go on a discovery into the mountain mining history of the Colline Metallifere, where the Etruscan got their riches from centuries ago. This includes a visit the mining museum and a trip on the small yellow train in a disused tunnel. *March–May and Oct Sat/Sun 10am–6pm, June and Sept Tue–Sun 10am–7pm, July/Aug daily 9.30am–7.30pm | 9 euros, children (6–14 years) 6 euros | www.parchival dicornia.it*

LUCCA, PISA & VERSILIA

GROTTA DEL VENTO NEAR
FORNOVOLASCO (135 E5) (*ⓜ D5–6*)
Stalactites, stalagmites, underground streams and lakes: discovered in the caves in the Apuan Alps on three comfortable and well-lit circular paths. *Daily 10am–7pm on the hour | depending on the tour 9/14/20 euros, children under 10 years 7/11/16 euros | www.grottadelvento.com*

MUSEO NAZIONALE DEL FUMETTO
IN LUCCA (136 C5) (*ⓜ E7*)
Somehow it is just logical that the Italian comic book museum is situated in Tuscany, because the Tuscans have been painting stories on church walls since the Middle Ages. Original drawings, life-size figures and scenes from contemporary picture books are exhibited in this former barracks. *Tue–Sun 10am–6pm | 4 euros, children 5–18 years 3 euros | Piazza San Romano 4 | www.museonazionaledelfumetto.com*

PARCO AVVENTURA IN FOSDINOVO
(134 C4) (*ⓜ B5*)
Fifty obstacles promise adventure for everyone: mountain bike course, a range for mini quads, swaying rope bridges and exciting zip lines. *March–mid June Sat/Sun 11am–5pm, mid June–mid Sept daily 10am–7pm, mid Sept–Oct daily 10am–5pm | 20 euros, youth 15 euros, children 8 euros | Via Cucco | www.parcoavventura fosdinovo.com*

FESTIVALS & EVENTS

Tuscans love to celebrate and there are festivals or tournaments for every occasion: a patron saint, a pagan custom, or an event in the city's history. A good option is a ● INSIDER TIP *sagra*, a local festival serving specialities, e.g the *Sagra della Birra* in Buriano at Grosseto in early August.

OFFICIAL HOLIDAYS

1 Jan; **6 Jan**; **Easter Monday**; **25 April** (*Liberazione* – anniversary of the liberation from German occupation) **1 May**; **2 June** (*Festa della Repubblica* – Republic Day); **15 Aug**; **1 Nov**; **8 Dec** (Immaculate Conception); **25/26 Dec**

EVENTS & FESTIVALS

FEBRUARY/MARCH
Highlight of the ▶ *carnival* are the allegorical papier mâché figures in Viareggio on the promenade. *www.viareggio.ilcarnevale.com*

MARCH/APRIL
The ▶ *Venerdì Santo* of Grassina (suburb of Florence) is the Tuscan version of the Passion play on Good Friday. *www.riev storicagrassina.it*

APRIL–MID JUNE
At the end of April the ▶ *Maggio Musicale Fiorentino,* the oldest music festival for modern classical music, starts in Florence. *www.maggiofiorentino.com*

MAY
On the last two Sundays of May, Lucignano in Arezzo, celebrates spring with a colourful ▶ INSIDER TIP flower carnival *Maggiolata*

JUNE
On the 17th of June, in Pisa is the ▶ *Regata di San Ranieri,* a race with historic rowing boats on the Arno River, and on the last Sunday in June, the ▶ *Gioco del Ponte:* on the Arno bridge Ponte di Mezzo, muscled men push a heavy trolley to the opposite side of the bridge.

At the ▶ *Calcio in Costume* in Florence on the 24th of June, three teams dressed in traditional costume fight over a ball. The day ends with a fireworks display. *www. calciostorico.it*

Sports, games, food, medieval tournaments or jazz concerts: Tuscan events come in many forms

JULY/AUGUST

The ▶ *Palio* in Siena (2 July, 16 Aug): ten riders on unsaddled horses race three times around the Piazza del Campo (it's over in about 100 seconds). *www.ilpalio.org*

The blues festival ▶ *Pistoia Blues* in July on the cathedral square.

▶ ● *Mercantia* in Certaldo (five days), street performers and artists show off their skills on the streets and squares. *www.mercantiacertaldo.it*

▶ *La Versiliana,* the multi-genre festival in Pietrasanta (mid-July to end of Aug), ideal for tourists who want a dash of culture. *www.laversilianafestival.com*

▶ *Effetto Venezia* is a nine day carnival at the end of July/early August in Livorno with music, dance, cabaret and folklore.

▶ *Grey Cat Festival:* You can hear the best jazz everywhere in the province of Grosseto. The historic game ▶ *Bravio delle Botti* on the last Sunday of August draws many visitors to Montepulciano. Wine barrels are rolled up the steep streets to the Piazza Grande. *www.braviodellebotti.com*

SEPTEMBER

The ▶ *Giostra del Saracino* in Arezzo (1st Sun) is a colourful costume festival, where riders have to hit a wooden figure with a lance. *www.giostradelsaracino.arezzo.it* Choirs from all over Europe travel to this acclaimed competition ▶ *Concorso Polifonico* in Arezzo during mid-September. *www.polifonico.org*

END OF OCTOBER

▶ *Lucca Comics & Games:* the name says it all. *www.luccacomicsandgames.com*

23–26 DECEMBER

At the ▶ *Presepe Vivente* in Equi Terme the locals enact the nativity. *www.presepeviventeequi.com*

LINKS, BLOGS, APPS & MORE

LINKS

▶ www.toscanainfesta.it This website lists the countless folk festivals that take place all over Tuscany. Many of which celebrate local culinary specialities such as the wild boar or mushroom festivals and there is even a doughnut festival

▶ www.atlantidephototravel.com Some excellent landscape photographs by three Florentine photographers to get you in the holiday mood. Simply enter 'Tuscany' in the search field

▶ www.discovertuscany.com This is a free online tourist resource written by a team of locals with lots of helpful information for your holiday. Reviews of accommodation, suggested destinations, an events calendar etc.

BLOGS & FORUMS

▶ www.toskana.net/blog/en Informative and appealing blog with articles, travel tips and listings for all the major towns in the Maremma region

▶ http://tuscany.angloinfo.com This blog is geared to expats living in Tuscany but it is also full of useful tourist tips with an events guide and a classified section

▶ www.ioamofirenze.com Want to know which restaurant is the coolest? The trendiest bar with the best evening aperitif? Where the next hot gig is? These are the kinds of topics discussed in the cult blog by a Florentine local. In English

Regardless of whether you are still preparing your trip or already in Tuscany: these addresses will provide you with more information, videos and networks to make your holiday even more enjoyable

VIDEOS

▶ www.youtube.com/watch?v=Ahqa Egl4hvw This is a short BBC clip about Tuscany's breathtaking scenery and delicious food

▶ www.youtube.com/visittuscany The Tuscan tourism website has an interactive map that allows you to select a village or town and then watch a video or you can choose from a number of different categories such as 'Seaside', 'Mountainside', 'Spa' etc.

APPS

▶ Tuscany Plus is the augmented reality app for iPhone (and soon for Android phones) that was created by the Tuscan Tourism Department. Load it on to your phone and hold the internal camera on a point, and a map appears with tags with information about sightseeing attractions, hotels and restaurants in the immediate vicinity

▶ Siena Walking Tours and Map/Pisa Walking Tours and Map is a good tool for the first stroll through either town as it offers one-hour tours that cover the culture, nightlife and shopping areas

▶ Florence Map and Walking Tours A great travel companion to help you to explore the city on foot, with a variety of talking tours each with a number of sights and a detailed city map

NETWORK

▶ www.talktotuscany.com Tripadvisor alla Tuscany, here Tuscany proves that it understands the interactive potential of the Internet. Visitors from around the world can visit the site and ask questions or post comments, tips and impressions

▶ www.couchsurfing.org Even if the accommodation aspect doesn't work out you can still use the site to chat to Tuscan locals and get some good insider tips

▶ www.i-escape.com A popular site with a portfolio of boutique hotels and guest houses to rent, the listings are usually independently owned, hip and stylish and offer something unusual

TRAVEL TIPS

ARRIVAL

Pisa's *Aeroporto Galileo Galilei* is the major airport hub in Tuscany and has good international links. From the airport there are regular, direct trains to Florence and to the other major Tuscan towns. Florence's airport, the *Aeroporto Amerigo Vespucci* lies just a few kilometers from the city.

The airport shuttle *Vola in Bus!* operates between 5.30am and 11pm and travels to the main railway station Santa Maria Novella. As Florence is actually only classed as a regional airport, there are few direct flights from the major European cities like London or Paris. Aside from Pisa and Florence, Rome is another entry airport for Tuscany.

When travelling by car the most comfortable route is to take the Brenner pass and the A 22 to Modena and from there further on the A 1 via Bologna to Florence. If you are travelling via Switzerland, take the A 1 in Milan to Modena, Bologna, Florence. An alternative is the stretch Milan–Parma, from there the A 15 and the Cisa pass to La Spezia and further towards Pisa. The motorways in Italy, Austria and Switzerland charge tolls. You can find the current toll prices at *www.autostrade.it/en/* keyword *tolls.*

From July until September trucks are banned from driving on the motorways during weekends.

Trains via Austria arrive in Florence via the Brenner and Bologna. Trains via Switzerland travel either on the Milan–Genova–Livorno–Grosseto route or the Milan–Bologna–Florence route. From Florence you can travel in any direction on the regional rail lines. Tickets are available at counters, vending machines or news-stands. However, you should know the distances before you make your purchase.

RESPONSIBLE TRAVEL

It doesn't take a lot to be environmentally friendly whilst travelling. Don't just think about your carbon footprint whilst flying to and from your holiday destination but also about how you can protect nature and culture abroad. As a tourist it is especially important to respect nature, look out for local products, cycle instead of driving, save water and much more. If you would like to find out more about eco-tourism please visit: *www.ecotourism.org*

ACCOMMODATION

AGRITURISMO

Hundreds of farms in Tuscany have guest rooms and apartments available for tourists. They range from simple rooms to suites on wine estates. They are rented out on a daily or weekly basis. Addresses with good offers can be found on website like *www.agriturismo.org.uk, www.terra nostra.it, www.agritour.net*

BED & BREAKFAST

On the website *www.bbitalia.it/default_eng.asp?* you will find numerous listings for private accommodation at attractive rates.

From arrival to weather

Holiday from start to finish: the most important addresses and information for your trip to Tuscany

CAMPING

Whether in the interior or on the coast, the quality of the camping sites has improved tremendously and is still very popular with families with children in Italy. *www.camping.it*

HOLIDAY ACCOMMODATION

These are some suggested website for you to browse prior to departure: *www.your tuscanvilla.com, www.holidayhomestus cany.com, www.homelidays.co.uk, www.tuscany.net*

HOTELS

In the tourist area along the coast or in the mountains you will often only find a room with half or full board during the high season. The prices skyrocket during August. During the low season many hotels have special offers.

ADMISSION FEES

Admission fees for museums and monuments vary widely. In the local tourist offices you can find out if there are any reduced admission tickets available and how or where you can book tickets in advance, in order to avoid long queues.

CAR & BICYCLE HIRE

Car rentals are available at all the airports and in the cities at the major companies. A credit card is obligatory. For a small car you will pay approx. 80 euros per day, weekly rates are cheaper. Booking prior to your trip is often cheaper, as are weekend specials. Vespa and motorcycle rental companies are also available in the major

holiday resorts. The Vespa, the legendary Italian scooter, takes some getting used to. Helmets are mandatory and are generally included in the price.

BUDGETING

Museum	£5.20/$8.50 *for the Uffizi in Florence*
Coffee	£1.20/$2 *for a cappuccino and standing at the bar counter*
Pizza	about £6.50/$10.50 *for a pizza in a restaurant*
Wine	about £3.20/$5.20 *for a glass of house wine*
Petrol	about £1.20/$2 *for Super unleaded*
Beach	about £20/$33 *per day to rent two deckchairs and an umbrella*

There are bicycle rentals at the main train station in Florence, otherwise you can ask at your hotel or at the local tourism information Pro Loco.

CLIMATE, WHEN TO GO

A temperate Mediterranean climate prevails in Tuscany and in the winter the sun shines often, however there are also cold and wet days. It normally only snows in the higher regions. Spring and autumn are the best times to travel. Travelling to

Tuscany in August is not ideal: the beaches are overcrowded and the cities are very hot and deserted.

CONSULATES & EMBASSIES

BRITISH EMBASSY ROME
Via XX Settembre 80a | I-00187 Roma RM | tel. +39 06 42 20 00 01 | ukinitaly.fco.gov.uk/en

US CONSULATE GENERAL FLORENCE
Lungarno Vespucci 38 | I-50123 Florence | tel. +39 05 5 26 69 51 | florence.usconsulate.gov

CANADIAN EMBASSY IN ROME
Via Zara 30 | I-00198 Rome | tel. +39 06 85 44 41 | www.canadainternational.gc.ca/italy-italie

CUSTOMS

UK citizens do not have to pay any duty on goods brought from another EU country as long as tax was included in the price and are for private consumption. The limits are: 800 cigarettes, 400 cigarillo, 200 cigars, 1kg tobacco, 10L spirits, 20L liqueurs, 90L wine, and 110L beer

Travellers from the USA, Canada, Australia or other non-EU countries are allowed to enter with the following tax-free amounts: 200 cigarettes or 100 cigarillos or 50 cigars or 250g tobacco, 2L wine, 2L spirits (under 22% vo.) and 1L spirits (over 22% vol.).

Travellers to the United States who are returning residents of the country do not have to pay duty on articles purchased overseas up to the value of $800, but there are limits on the amount of alcoholic beverages and tobacco products. For the regulations for international travel for U.S. residents please see *http://www.cbp.gov*

DRIVING

On the motorways the maximum speed is 130km/h or 80mi/h and in suburban areas 90km/h or 55mi/h. The alcohol

CULTURAL SUMMER IN TUSCANY

Rural migration hit many villages in the 1960s including Monticchiello near Pienza. The young people left, houses stood empty and the land lay fallow. The people who were left behind were anxious that their homes would be taken over by affluent city dwellers and newcomers. But then they discovered drama as their way to resist fate and to give new cohesion to their village. Every year since 1967, in late July or early August, the people of Monticchiello perform a play they wrote about their life in Tuscany to great success! The *Teatro Povero*, the 'poor theatre', is just one of many highlights of the Tuscan cultural summer. Between May and September a piazza or park, a cloister or a church, a neighbourhood or a street are declared cultural areas. Where dance or theatre, film or music – sometimes traditional, sometimes avant-garde – are performed. Some of these initiatives are well established, including the theatre festival *Volterrateatro*, the Maremma jazz festival, the *Grey Cat Festival* or Pelago's *On The Road Festival*, near Florence, where street artists perform in June.

limit is 0.5 and talking on a mobile phone whilst driving is prohibited. Outside of towns the cars dipped-beam headlamps must always be on, and in case of an accident or breakdown you have to wear a reflective vest when leaving your car.

Petrol stations are open on weekdays from 7.30am to 12.30pm and 3pm to 7pm, Sundays only at certain arterial roads and along the motorways. There are self-service machines everywhere and they are usually open 24 hours.

You have to pay toll on the motorways, but they are recommended for longer trips because the regional roads often run through hilly, mountainous regions and are often slow and winding. A toll road is also being planned for both the Tuscan motorways Florence–Siena–Grosseto and Florence–Pisa–Livorno.

If you see the sign ZTL (Zona a Traffico Limitato) at the entrance to the historic downtown areas this indicates that only vehicles with permission are allowed access. This applies to most vehicles in almost all the inner cities and car parks on the outskirts are expensive. If you have booked into a hotel in the old town there is usually a residential parking permit. You may also have to move the car from the inner city after you have unloaded your luggage. Only hotels with three stars or more have private garages or parking areas. And only residents are allowed to park on the road. Parking discs suffice for blue marked parking spots or else be on the lookout for parking ticket machines. For longer stays it is more convenient to use the paid parking garages and parking lots which almost every town has within close proximity of the sites (approx. 1–2 euros per hour). If you are planning a trip to another town, it is best to use public transport where possible and the bus and the train network goes almost everywhere. But if you want to spend the even-

CURRENCY CONVERTER

£	€	€	£
1	1.30	1	0.80
3	3.80	3	2.40
5	6.30	5	4
13	16.30	13	10
40	50	40	32
75	94	75	60
120	150	120	96
250	313	250	200
500	625	500	400

$	€	€	$
1	0.80	1	1.30
3	2.30	3	3.90
5	3.80	5	6.50
13	10	13	11
40	30.80	40	52
75	58	75	98
120	92	120	156
250	192	250	325
500	385	500	650

For current exchange rates see www.xe.com

ing rather take your own vehicle as there are hardly any busses or trains after 10pm.

ELECTRICITY

The power supply complies with European Union norms standards. It is advisable to carry an adapter for the plugs.

EMERGENCY SERVICES

Carabinieri (for crime) *tel. 112;* Fire brigade *(Vigili del fuoco) tel. 115;* Emergency doctor and ambulance *tel. 118;* Police (for accidents or emergency doctor) *tel. 113* Breakdown assistance *tel. 80 3116*

HEALTH

If you are a UK or European Union resident your free European Health Insurance Card (EHIC) will allow you access to medical treatment while travelling. If you are treated at a private practise or private clinic you have to pay upfront and then claim from your insurance on your return home. Private medical travel insurance is recommended. The hospital ambulances *(pronto soccorso)* are generally very fast and good.

IMMIGRATION

Citizens of the UK & Ireland, USA, Canada, Australia and New Zealand need only a valid passport to enter all countries of the EU. Children below the age of 12 need a children's passport.

INFORMATION

ITALIAN GOVERNMENT TOURIST BOARD
– *1 Princes St. | London W1B 2AY | tel. 020 74 08 12 54 | www.italiantourist board.co.uk*
– *630 Fifth Avenue | New York NY 10111| tel. 212 245 48 22 | www.italiantourism.com*
– *110 Yonge Street East Suite 503 | Toronto ON M5C IT4 | tel. 416 925 48 82 | e-mail: toronto@enit.it*

WWW.TURISMO.INTOSCANA.IT
The official website for the Tuscany region has lots of information and many links to other sites.

INVOICES & RECEIPTS

For all services and goods you have to ask for receipts in Italy *(scontrino)* and these must be kept to show to the tax authorities *(Guardia di Finanzia)* who conduct frequent spot-checks.

MONEY & CREDIT CARDS

Almost all the banks have ATMs or *banco-mat* and many restaurants, hotels and shops as well as fuel stations accept credit cards. Banks are generally open as follows: *Mon–Fri 8.20am–1.20pm and 2.45pm–3.45pm*.

MUSEUMS

The large state museums are closed on Mondays, but some are open with curtailed hours. Admission is free for EU citizens under the age of 18 and over the age of 65. For ages 18 to 25 admission is half price.

OPENING HOURS

Lunchtime is still sacred in Tuscany. Smaller shops are generally open from 9am to 1pm and then from 4pm to 7.30pm. They are also closed on Sundays and Monday mornings. Many large supermarkets and shopping centres are open from 8am to 8pm, sometimes even on Sundays. Churches are mostly closed over lunch. No sightseeing is allowed during services.

PHONE & MOBILE PHONE

The international dialling code for Italy is *0039* and the area code is part of the number and must always be dialled (including the zero). Dial *0044* for calls from Italy to the UK and *001* from Italy to the USA. Mobile numbers start without a zero. To make calls from a foreign mobile telephone it is cheaper to use an Italian prepaid card. They are sold in tobacco shops for 5–10 euros. For frequent callers it is worthwhile buying a rechargeable SIM card from one of the four service providers (Wind, Vodafone, Telecom, Fastweb). You can then have an Italian number and the charges for incoming calls are dropped.

When buying a SIM you have to have proof of identity, a contact address and a mobile phone. There are only a few public telephones that use coins. Telephone cards *(carta telefonica)* are available in bars, tobacco shops and post offices.

POLICE

In typical Italian fashion there are several categories of police: the *Vigili* or *Polizia Municipale* are traffic police while the *Carabinieri* and *Polizia di Stato* are responsible for criminal offences. The railway police are called *Polfer* and tax investigators are the *Guardia di Finanza.* They are all allowed to ask for your passport.

PUBLIC TRANSPORT

Regional public transport is comparatively inexpensive and the intercity buses and trains are fairly punctual. They run often during the day and less frequently at night. The fast Eurostar train that connects large cities is more expensive and reservations are essential. However, you can save some money by purchasing your tickets a few weeks in advance. Train tickets without reservations must be validated at the station. From Florence the intercity bus lines go to almost all the places in Tuscany. Tickets for the city bus can be bought from news-stands or in tobacco shops, for intercity buses you can buy from your departure point and in the bars near the bus stops. A surcharge of 1 euro is payable on the bus.

SMOKING

Smoking is now strictly prohibited in all public indoor places, those who violate the regulations may be fined up to 250 euros.

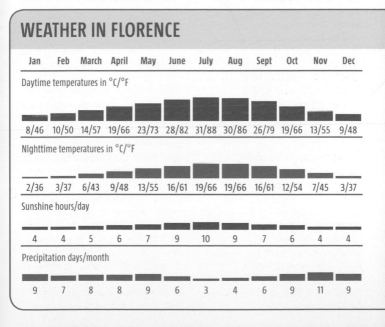

WEATHER IN FLORENCE

	Jan	Feb	March	April	May	June	July	Aug	Sept	Oct	Nov	Dec
Daytime temperatures in °C/°F	8/46	10/50	14/57	19/66	23/73	28/82	31/88	30/86	26/79	19/66	13/55	9/48
Nighttime temperatures in °C/°F	2/36	3/37	6/43	9/48	13/55	16/61	19/66	19/66	16/61	12/54	7/45	3/37
Sunshine hours/day	4	4	5	6	7	9	10	9	7	6	4	4
Precipitation days/month	9	7	8	8	9	6	3	4	6	9	11	9

USEFUL PHRASES ITALIAN

PRONUNCIATION

c, cc	before e or i like ch in "church", e.g. ciabatta, otherwise like k
ch, cch	like k, e.g. pacchi, che
g, gg	before e or i like j in "just", e.g. gente, otherwise like g in "get"
gl	like "lli" in "million", e.g. figlio
gn	as in "cognac", e.g. bagno
sc	before e or i like sh, e.g. uscita
sch	like sk in "skill", e.g. Ischia
z	at the beginning of a word like dz in "adze", otherwise like ts

An accent on an Italian word shows that the stress is on the last syllable.
In other cases we have shown which syllable is stressed by placing a dot below the relevant vowel.

IN BRIEF

Yes/No/Maybe	Sì/No/Forse
Please/Thank you	Per favore/Grazie
Excuse me, please!	Scusa!/Mi scusi
May I ...?/Pardon?	Posso ...? / Come dice?/Prego?
I would like to .../Have you got ...?	Vorrei .../Avete ...?
How much is ...?	Quanto costa ...?
I (don't) like that	(Non) mi piace
good/bad	buono/cattivo/bene/male
broken/doesn't work	guasto/non funziona
too much/much/little/all/nothing	troppo/molto/poco/ tutto/niente
Help!/Attention!/Caution!	aiuto!/attenzione!/prudenza!
ambulance/police/fire brigade	ambulanza/polizia/vigili del fuoco
Prohibition/forbidden/danger/dangerous	divieto/vietato/pericolo/pericoloso
May I take a photo here/of you?	Posso fotografar La?

GREETINGS, FAREWELL

Good morning!/afternoon!/ evening!/night!	Buon giorno!/Buon giorno!/ Buona sera!/Buona notte!
Hello! / Goodbye!/See you	Ciao!/Salve! / Arrivederci!/Ciao!
My name is ...	Mi chiamo ...
What's your name?	Come si chiama?/Come ti chiami
I'm from ...	Vengo da ...

Parli italiano?

"Do you speak Italian?" This guide will help you to say the basic words and phrases in Italian

DATE & TIME

Monday/Tuesday/Wednesday	lunedì/martedì/mercoledì
Thursday/Friday/Saturday	giovedì/venerdì/sabato
Sunday/holiday/	domenica/(giorno) festivo/
working day	(giorno) feriale
today/tomorrow/yesterday	oggi/domani/ieri
hour/minute	ora/minuto
day/night/week/month/year	giorno/notte/settimana/mese/anno
What time is it?	Che ora è? Che ore sono?
It's three o'clock/It's half past three	Sono le tre/Sono le tre e mezza
a quarter to four	le quattro meno un quarto/
	un quarto alle quattro

TRAVEL

open/closed	aperto/chiuso
entrance/exit	entrata/uscita
departure/arrival	partenza/arrivo
toilets/ladies/gentlemen	bagno/toilette/signore/signori
(no) drinking water	acqua (non) potabile
Where is ...?/Where are ...?	Dov'è ...?/Dove sono ...?
left/right/straight ahead/back	sinistra/destra/dritto/indietro
close/far	vicino/lontano
bus/tram	bus/tram
taxi/cab	taxi/tassì
bus stop/cab stand	fermata/posteggio taxi
parking lot/parking garage	parcheggio/parcheggio coperto
street map/map	pianta/mappa
train station/harbour	stazione/porto
airport	aeroporto
schedule/ticket	orario/biglietto
supplement	supplemento
single/return	solo andata/andata e ritorno
train/track	treno/binario
platform	banchina/binario
I would like to rent ...	Vorrei noleggiare ...
a car/a bicycle	una macchina/una bicicletta
a boat	una barca
petrol/gas station	distributore/stazione di servizio
petrol/gas / diesel	benzina/diesel/gasolio
breakdown/repair shop	guasto/officina

FOOD & DRINK

Could you please book a table for tonight for four?	Vorrei prenotare per stasera un tavolo per quattro?
on the terrace/by the window	sulla terrazza/ vicino alla finestra
The menu, please	La carta/il menù, per favore
Could I please have ...?	Potrei avere ...?
bottle/carafe/glass	bottiglia/caraffa/bicchiere
knife/fork/spoon/salt/pepper	coltello/forchetta/cucchiaio/sale/pepe
sugar/vinegar/oil/milk/cream/lemon	zucchero/aceto/olio/latte/panna/limone
cold/too salty/not cooked	freddo/troppo salato/non cotto
with/without ice/sparkling	con/senza ghiaccio/gas
vegetarian/allergy	vegetariano/vegetariana/allergia
May I have the bill, please?	Vorrei pagare/Il conto, per favore
bill/tip	conto/mancia

SHOPPING

Where can I find...?	Dove posso trovare ...?
I'd like .../I'm looking for ...	Vorrei .../Cerco ...
Do you put photos onto CD?	Vorrei masterizzare delle foto su CD?
pharmacy/shopping centre/kiosk	farmacia/centro commerciale/edicola
department store/supermarket	grandemagazzino/supermercato
baker/market/grocery	forno/ mercato/negozio alimentare
photographic items/newspaper shop/	articoli per foto/giornalaio
100 grammes/1 kilo	un etto/un chilo
expensive/cheap/price/more/less	caro/economico/prezzo/di più/di meno
organically grown	di agricoltura biologica

ACCOMMODATION

I have booked a room	Ho prenotato una camera
Do you have any ... left?	Avete ancora ...
single room/double room	una (camera) singola/doppia
breakfast/half board/	prima colazione/mezza pensione/
full board (American plan)	pensione completa
at the front/seafront/lakefront	con vista/con vista sul mare/lago
shower/sit-down bath/balcony/terrace	doccia/bagno/balcone/terrazza
key/room card	chiave/scheda magnetica
luggage/suitcase/bag	bagaglio/valigia/borsa

BANKS, MONEY & CREDIT CARDS

bank/ATM/pin code	banca/bancomat/ codice segreto
cash/credit card	in contanti/carta di credito
bill/coin/change	banconota/moneta/il resto

HEALTH

doctor/dentist/paediatrician	medico/dentista/pediatra
hospital/emergency clinic	ospedale/pronto soccorso/guardia medica
fever/pain/inflamed/injured	febbre/dolori/infiammato/ferito
diarrhoea/nausea/sunburn	diarrea/nausea/scottatura solare
plaster/bandage/ointment/cream	cerotto/fasciatura/pomata/crema
pain reliever/tablet/suppository	antidolorifico/compressa/supposta

POST, TELECOMMUNICATIONS & MEDIA

stamp/letter/postcard	francobollo/lettera/cartolina
I need a landline phone card/ I'm looking for a prepaid card for my mobile	Mi serve una scheda telefonica per la rete fissa/Cerco una scheda prepagata per il mio cellulare
Where can I find internet access?	Dove trovo un accesso internet?
dial/connection/engaged	comporre/linea/occupato
socket/adapter/charger	presa/riduttore/caricabatterie
computer/battery/rechargeable battery	computer/batteria/accumulatore
internet address (URL)/e-mail address	indirizzo internet/indirizzo email
internet connection/wifi	collegamento internet/wi-fi
e-mail/file/print	email/file/stampare

LEISURE, SPORTS & BEACH

beach/bathing beach	spiaggia/bagno/stabilimento balneare
sunshade/lounger/cable car/chair lift	ombrellone/sdraio/funivia/seggiovia
(rescue) hut/avalanche	rifugio/valanga

NUMBERS

0	zero	15	quindici
1	uno	16	sedici
2	due	17	diciassette
3	tre	18	diciotto
4	quattro	19	diciannove
5	cinque	20	venti
6	sei	21	ventuno
7	sette	50	cinquanta
8	otto	100	cento
9	nove	200	duecento
10	dieci	1000	mille
11	undici	2000	duemila
12	dodici	10000	diecimila
13	tredici	½	un mezzo
14	quattordici	¼	un quarto

NOTES

FOR YOUR NEXT HOLIDAY ...

MARCO POLO TRAVEL GUIDES

MARCO POLO
With ROAD ATLAS & PULL-OUT MAP
FRENCH RIVIERA
NICE, CANNES & MONACO
SPECTACULAR GRAND CANYON DU VERDON
Breath-taking scenery that takes some beating
SNIFFING THE AIR
The perfume manufacturers of Grasse
Insider Tips
www.marco-polo.com

MARCO POLO
With STREET ATLAS & PULL-OUT MAP
NEW YORK
MEADOWS, WILD FLOWERS AND SKYSCRAPERS
Green is chic: the High Line in Chelsea
COCKTAIL ON CLOUD NINE
Rooftop bar at 230 Fifth Street
Insider Tips

MARCO POLO
With ROAD ATLAS & PULL-OUT MAP
AKE GARDA
TE BALDO WITH MOUNTAIN BIKE
air in Malcesine takes bikes too
KISSES" IN SALÒ
hocolate "Baceri"
Insider Tips

MARCO POLO
With STREET ATLAS & PULL-OUT MAP
BERLIN
A STUNNING ISLAND JUST FOR ART
Showcasing treasures from around the world
COOL AT NIGHT
tin club scene sets the trend
Insider Tips
www.marco-polo.com

MARCO POLO
With ROAD ATLAS & PULL-OUT MAP
ALLORCA
AN FLAIR IN THE MEDITERRANEAN
llorca's most beautiful beach
IN" CROWD MEET
enta in Deià
Insider Tips

- PACKED WITH INSIDER TIPS
- BEST WALKS AND TOURS
- FULL-COLOUR PULL-OUT MAP
  AND STREET ATLAS

ROAD ATLAS

The green line [   ] indicates the Trips & Tours (p. 102–107)
The blue line [   ] indicates The perfect route (p. 30–31)

All tours are also marked on the pull-out map

Photo: Maremma near Magliano

Exploring Tuscany

The map on the back cover shows how the area has been sub-divided

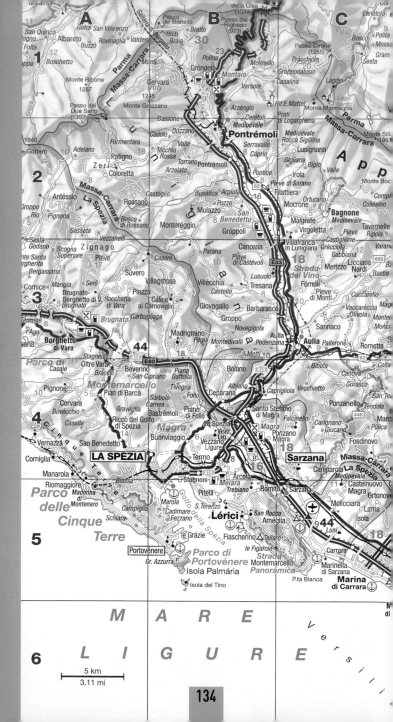

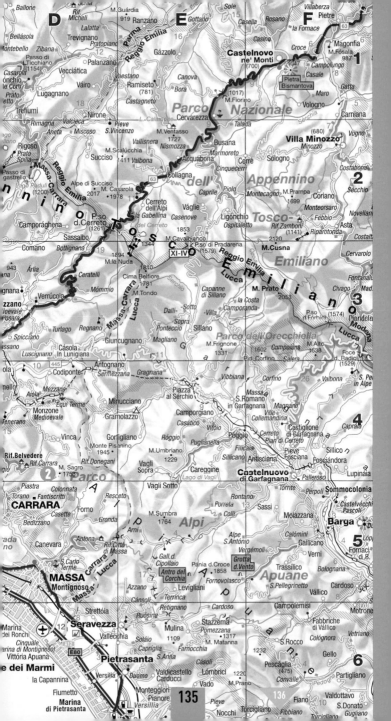

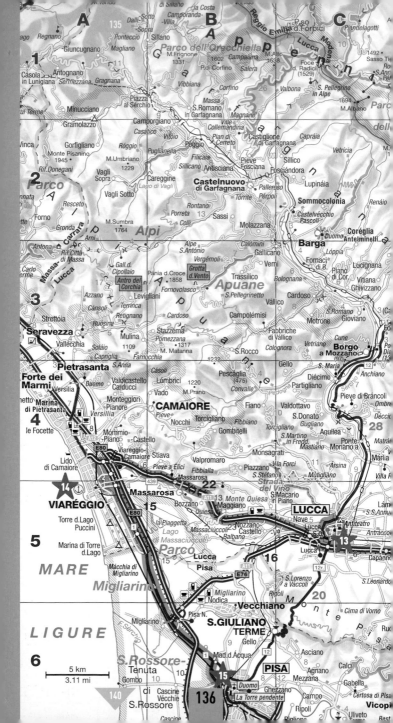

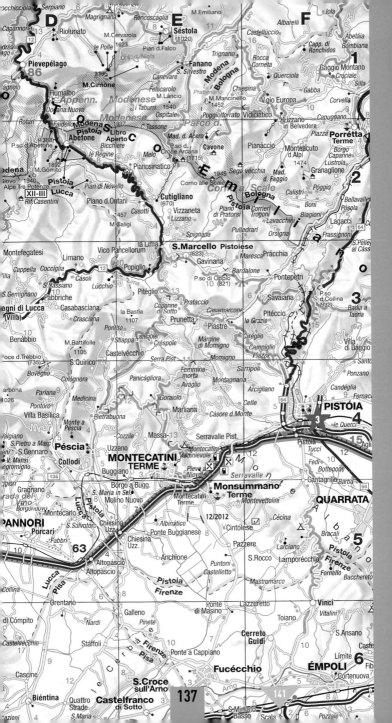

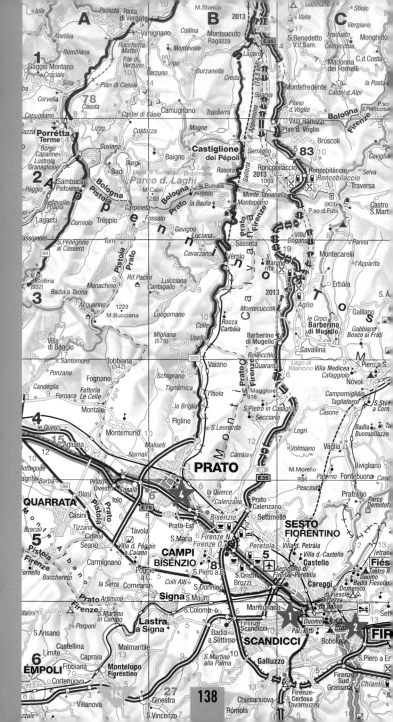

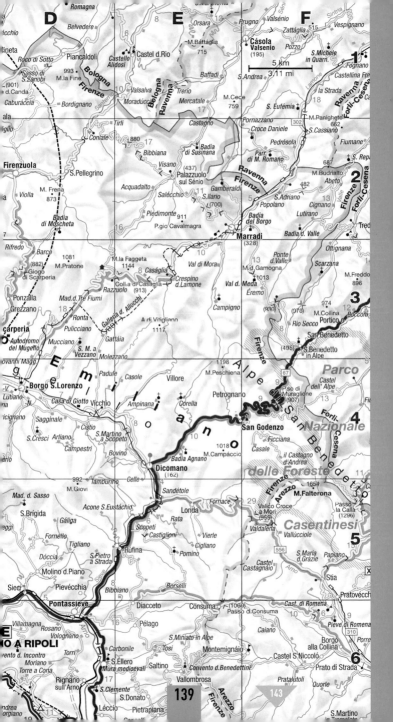

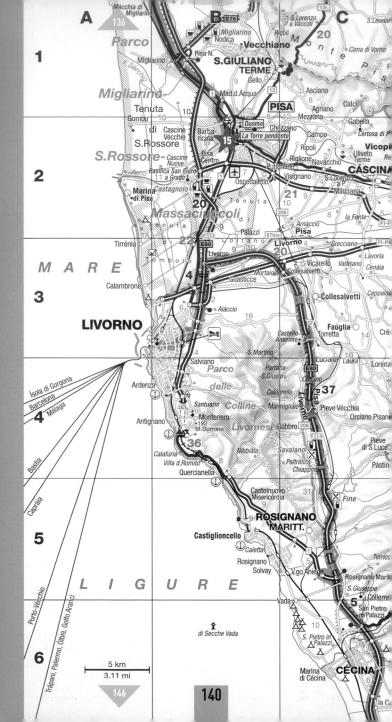

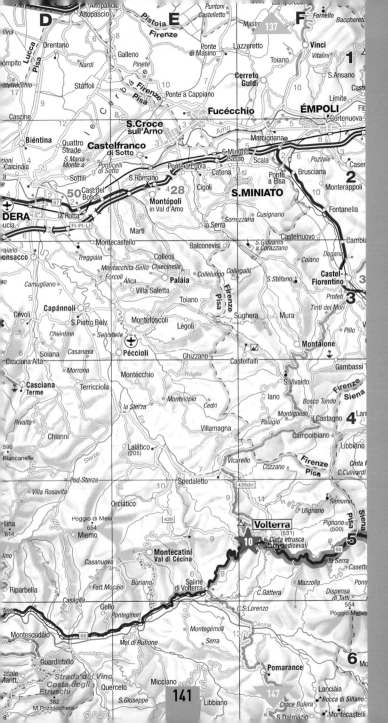

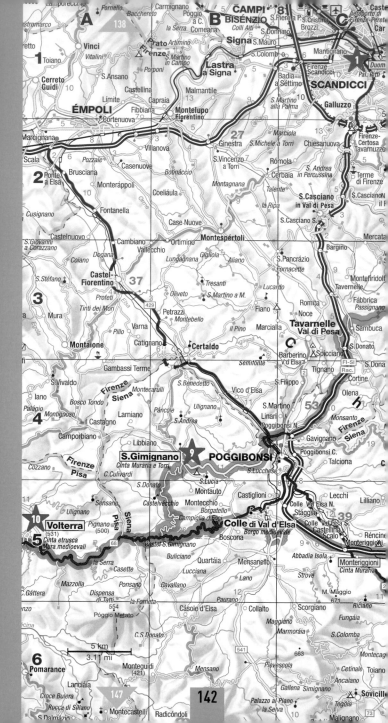

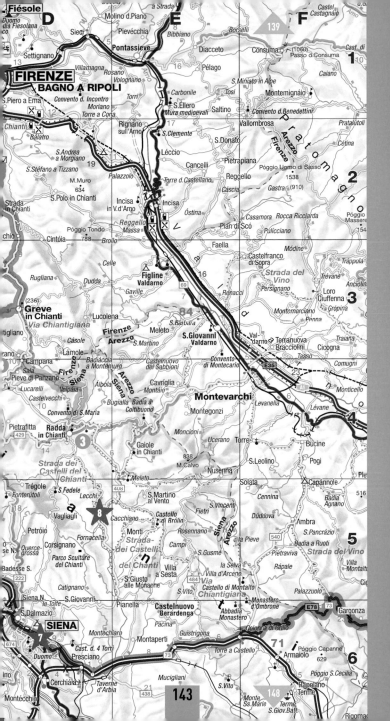

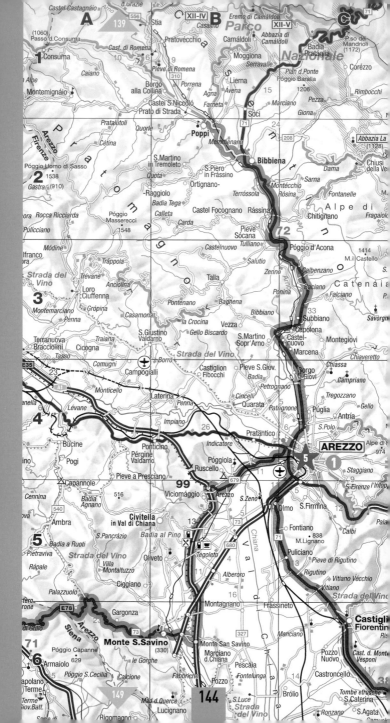

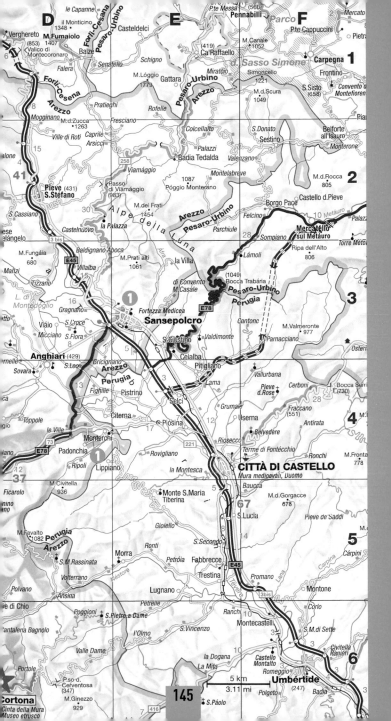

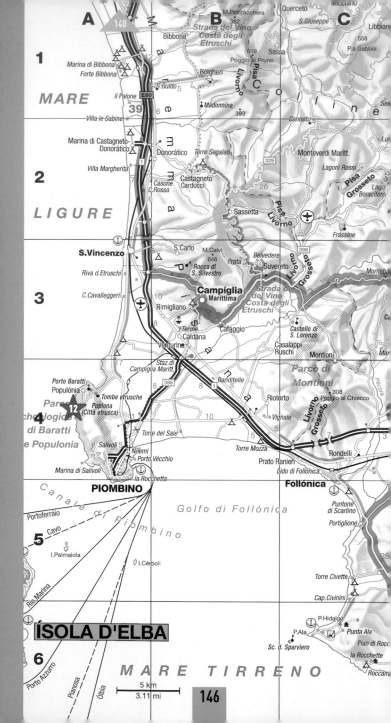

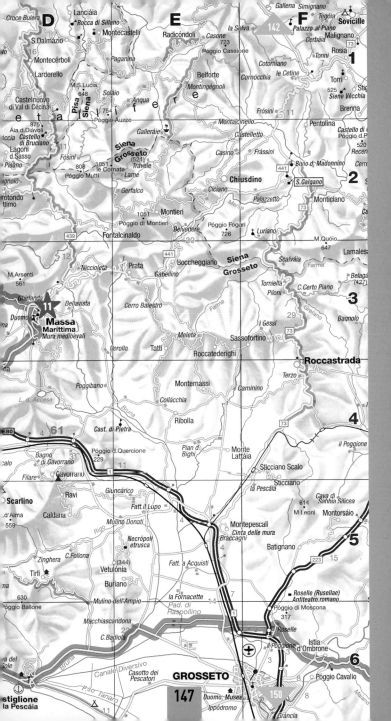

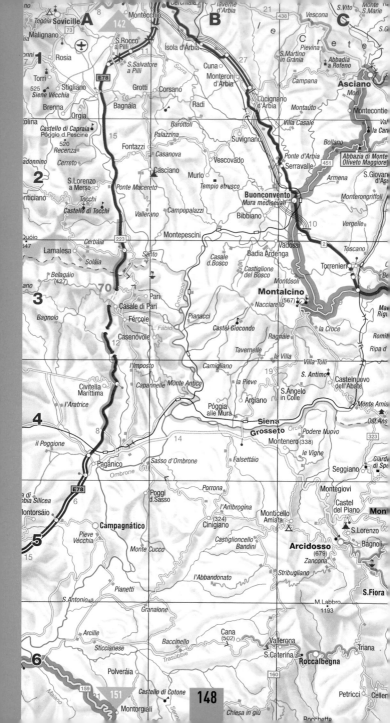

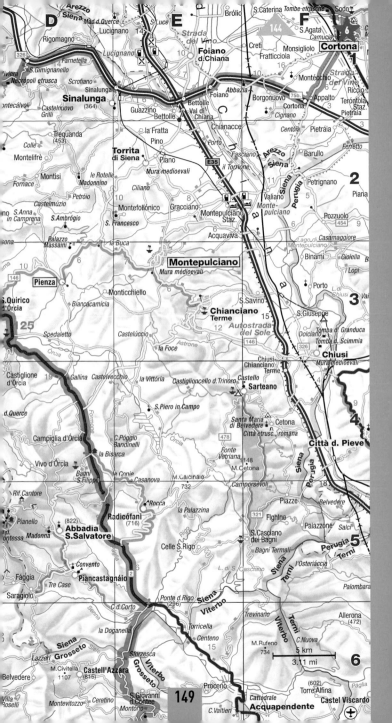

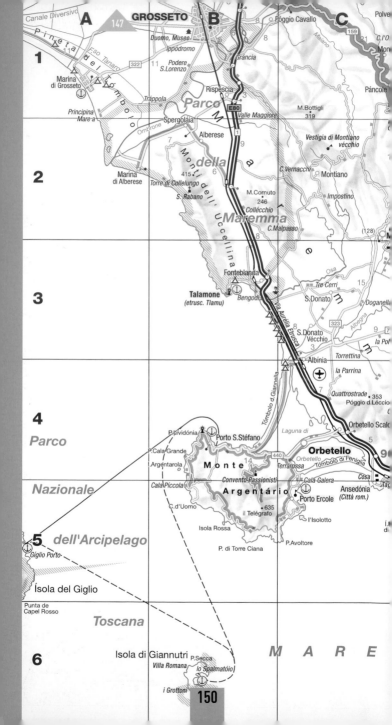

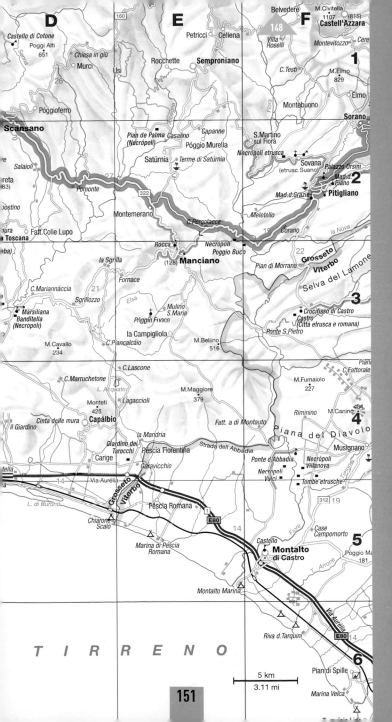

KEY TO ROAD ATLAS

English	Symbol	Deutsch
Motorway with junction and junction number	Idstein · Viernheim	Autobahn mit Anschlussstelle und Anschlussnummer
Motorway under construction with expected date of opening	Datum · Date	Autobahn in Bau mit voraussichtlichem Fertigstellungsdatum
Hotel, motel · Restaurant	Kassel	Rasthaus mit Übernachtung · Raststätte
Snackbar · Filling-station		Kiosk · Tankstelle
Truckstop · Parking place with WC	P	Autohof · Parkplatz mit WC
Toll station		Autobahn-Gebührenstelle
Dual carriageway with motorway characteristics		Autobahnähnliche Schnellstraße
Trunk road		Fernverkehrsstraße
Main road		Verbindungsstraße
Secondary roads		Nebenstraßen
Carriageway · Footpath		Fahrweg · Fußweg
Toll road		Gebührenpflichtige Straße
Road closed for motor vehicles	X X X X X	Straße für Kraftfahrzeuge gesperrt
Road closed for caravans		Straße für Wohnanhänger gesperrt
Road not recommended for caravans		Straße für Wohnanhänger nicht empfehlenswert
Car ferry · Autorail station		Autofähre · Autozug-Terminal
Main line railway · Station · Tunnel		Hauptbahn · Bahnhof · Tunnel
Cultural site of particular interest	Neuschwanstein	Besonders sehenswertes kulturelles Objekt
Landscape of particular interest	Breitachklamm	Besonders sehenswertes landschaftliches Objekt
Trips & Tours		Ausflüge & Touren
Perfect route		Perfekte Route
MARCO POLO Highlight	★1	MARCO POLO Highlight
Route with beautiful scenery		Landschaftlich schöne Strecke
Tourist route	Hanse-Route	Touristenstraße
Tourist train		Museumseisenbahn
Church, chapel · Church ruin Monastery · Monastery ruin		Kirche, Kapelle · Kirchenruine Kloster · Klosterruine
Palace, castle · Castle ruin Tower · Radio or TV tower		Schloss, Burg · Burgruine Turm · Funk-, Fernsehturm
Lighthouse · Windmill Monument · Military cemetery		Leuchtturm · Windmühle Denkmal · Soldatenfriedhof
Archaeological excavation, ruins · Cave Hotel, inn, refuge · Spa		Ruine, frühgeschichtliche Stätte · Höhle Hotel, Gasthaus, Berghütte · Heilbad
Camping site · Youth hostel Swimming pool, leisure pool, beach · Golf-course		Campingplatz · Jugendherberge Schwimmbad, Erlebnisbad, Strandbad · Golfplatz
Botanical gardens, interesting park · Zoological garden		Botanischer Garten, sehenswerter Park · Zoologischer Garten
Important building · Important area		Bedeutendes Bauwerk · Bedeutendes Areal
Airport · Regional airport		Verkehrsflughafen · Regionalflughafen
Airfield · Gliding site		Flugplatz · Segelflugplatz
Marina		Boots- und Jachthafen

INDEX

WRITE TO US

e-mail: info@marcopologuides.co.uk

Did you have a great holiday?
Is there something on your mind?
Whatever it is, let us know!
Whether you want to praise, alert us
to errors or give us a personal tip –
MARCO POLO would be pleased to
hear from you.
We do everything we can to provide the
very latest information for your trip.

Nevertheless, despite all of our authors'
thorough research, errors can creep in.
MARCO POLO does not accept any
liability for this. Please contact us by
e-mail or post.

MARCO POLO Travel Publishing Ltd
Pinewood, Chineham Business Park
Crockford Lane, Chineham
Basingstoke, Hampshire RG24 8AL
United Kingdom

PICTURE CREDITS
Cover photograph: farmhouse near Pienza (Look: Martini)
C. Büld Campetti (1 bottom); DuMont Bildarchiv (30 left), Widmann (112/113, 116); ©fotolia.com: Nina Hoff (17 top); Huber: Borchi (6, 108/109), Carassale (26 right), Cellai (42, 100), Cenadelli (118 top), Cozzi (74/75), Da Ros Luca (3 top, 70/71, 88), Dutton (8), Friedel (72), Gräfenhain (front flap right, 15, 40), Johanna Huber (78), Klaes (3 centre, 84/85), Rellini (83, 153), Ripani (18/19, 30 right), Scattolin (132/133), Giovanni Simeone (2 top, 4, 10/11), Spila (107); R Irek (118 bottom); ©iStockphoto.com: fatmayilmaz (16 top), gerenme (17 bottom); M. Kirchgessner (63, 94); Laif: Eid (27, 44); L'ANDANA – Tenuta La Badiola: Giovanni Cecchinato (16 centre); Look: Martini (1 top); mauritius images: Alamy (2 centre top, 7, 9, 38, 48, 51, 93, 99, 114), Friedmann (117), Harding (110), United Archives (20); H. P. Merten (front flap left, 34, 61); D. Renckhoff (23, 28, 28/29, 64); M. Schulte-Kellinghaus (2 centre bottom, 2 bottom, 26 left, 32/33, 52/53, 67, 86); Spiegelhalter: Schulte-Kellinghaus (29, 56); O. Stadler (3 bottom, 5, 12/13, 24/25, 37, 76/77, 102/103, 105, 119); M. Thomas (47); Villa Fontelunga (16 bottom); I. P. Widmann (54, 58, 69, 80, 90, 97, 116/117)

1st Edition 2013
Worldwide Distribution: Marco Polo Travel Publishing Ltd, Pinewood, Chineham Business Park, Crockford Lane, Basingstoke, Hampshire RG24 8AL, United Kingdom. Email: sales@marcopolouk.com
© MAIRDUMONT GmbH & Co. KG, Ostfildern
Chief editors: Michaela Lienemann (concept, managing editor), Marion Zorn (concept, text editor)
Author: Christiane Büld Campetti; editor: Nikolai Michaelis
Programme supervision: Anita Dahlinger, Ann-Katrin Kutzner, Nikolai Michaelis
Picture editor: Gabriele Forst
What's hot: wunder media, Munich
Cartography road atlas & pull-out map: © MAIRDUMONT, Ostfildern
Design: milchhof : atelier, Berlin; Front cover, pull-out map cover, page 1: factor product munich
Translated from German by Wendy Barrow; editor of the English edition: Margaret Howie, fullproof.co.za
Prepress: M. Feuerstein, Wigel
Phrase book in cooperation with Ernst Klett Sprachen GmbH, Stuttgart, Editorial by Pons Wörterbücher

DOS & DON'TS ☝

A few things to look out on your holiday

DO AVOID FAKES

Even if you are an avid bargain hunter: do not buy anything – cheap Ray Bans, Gucci handbags, Louis Vuitton purses – from the *vu cumpra*, street hawkers from Senegal or Somalia that ply the pedestrian zones. The goods are never the real thing and as it is illegal to purchase them if caught you can be fined up to 3000 euros.

DO PAY YOUR WAY ON THE TRAIN

The excuse that you are a stranger to the country and do not understand how the system works will not fly here. Do not forget to validate your ticket prior to a train or bus ride. The stamping machines are in the train stations or on the platforms.

DON'T MAKE SPONTANEOUS VISITS TO MUSEUMS

Do not plan a visit to any of the large museums, like the Uffizi in Florence, without making reservations beforehand. It might cost you a few euros extra but it will save having to wait in long queues.

DON'T BE TOO CAREFREE

It is an unfortunate fact that you need to be on the lookout for children who beg. They often have a newspaper in their one hand and thus obscure the other hand so that they have it free to pickpocket.

DO REMEMBER TO ASK FOR A RECEIPT

Always remember to take your receipt with you, even if you only had a coffee in a bar. The only exceptions are newspapers, petrol and cigarettes. The *scontrino* is the proof that the product or service has been paid for and taxes are paid. Tax investigators might carry out spot checks and if you have no receipt it can be very expensive for you and the seller.

DO DRESS APPROPRIATELY

In Italy it is expected that appropriate clothing (no shorts, no skimpy tops) be worn in churches and places of worship. It is also best not to walk around talking and taking photographs while religious services are in progress.

DO OBEY TRAFFIC RULES

Illegal parking, driving over the speed limit, driving under the influence of alcohol or talking on the phone without a hands-free set are all infringements that can be very expensive as the fines in Italy are amongst the highest in Europe.